MW00439635

MORE THAN EVERYTHING

a memoir

Vanessa G. Foster

25jumpingjacks Books

PUBLISHER'S NOTE
This memoir is a work of non-fiction; however, some
names have been changed.

Published in the United States of America

25jumpingjacks Books

A SIN: BOOBJMV23M
ISBN-13: 978-0615780870
ISBN-10: 0615780873

Memoir/Women/Relationships/Abuse/True Story

Photographs are courtesy of the author.

Jacket photograph and design by Vanessa G. Foster.
Boots purchased at the Red Wing store, Anchorage,
Alaska, July 1985

www.about.me/vgfoster

For my daughter,
Shalyn with all my love.

PREFACE

The stories in these pages occurred in my life between 1978 and 1988. I began writing this book in 1991 in an effort to sort through everything that had happened, to examine my decisions, and to reconcile the "me" that came out the other side of it all with the misguided young woman in these pages. The memories were still fresh then, and I had my journals to refer to. What I had written in those pages proved invaluable in piecing together a cohesive book. Through multiple iterations, I settled on first person, present tense for many reasons; namely, upon stumbling on this combination accidentally, deeper memories were triggered, and the words really began to flow.

My deepest hope is that *More Than Everything* will be encouraging to young women everywhere who find themselves in seemingly impossible situations, and that they too will find a way out and come to understand that the right thing to do is usually the toughest one at the time.

ACKNOWLEDGEMENTS

It took me 20 years to write my story and still more time to decide to publish it. The process has been gut-wrenching and cathartic and I could not have finished it without the loving support of my family and friends, and especially my husband, Ken, whose encouragement and feedback have been invaluable.

Life can only be understood backwards;
but it must be lived forwards.
~ Soren Kierkegaard

MORE THAN EVERYTHING

Shane and Vanessa, circa 1983

Chapter One

It is the summer of 1985 and I am working on a cattle ranch in Alaska for room and board. I am the cook. I can barely comprehend the series of events that have brought me here and there is no time to think about it anyway. I'm pretty sure God is keeping me busy so I won't dwell on the craziness I endured before arriving in this magical place.

I don't really know how to cook, but that's ok because there are angels in this kitchen teaching me what to do with the fresh salmon, halibut and crab, the freezer full of moose steaks and roasts, and the fresh vegetables from the plentiful garden. They whisper into my ears that I should squeeze some lemon on the halibut sizzling in the pan, filling the room with mouthwatering aromas. They gently nudge me toward the paprika and tell me how much to sprinkle onto the thick, pink salmon steaks before placing them in the broiler. Through them I know just how much salt a moose steak requires, how much pepper. My body moves around the kitchen looking confident but I am only a puppet. The angels are in charge and it is exhilarating. And I continue to trust them because everything tastes perfect. Yesterday I was a frightened young woman whose kitchen experience had been limited to few basics learned as a child while sitting on the kitchen counter watching mama fix dinner; now the kitchen seems constantly filled with mouthwatering aromas and I am feeding five (sometimes more) people delicious, nutritious meals three times a day.

The angels do not show themselves to me but I imagine one who is jolly and round, wearing a puffy chef's cap, instructing me on every nuance of the day's entrée; one with large, warm bread-doughy hands who embraces me with all the knowledge of breads, cakes, and pies; and one who is thin and efficient with sparkly blue eyes who specializes in enthusiastic side dishes. Together they slice, dice, mix, knead, boil, braze and bake through me with joyful exuberance. Each perfect meal is like a miracle to me and the miracles fill me up until I think I might burst with pride and joy. It has been a long time since I have done anything to be proud about.

Shane and I go hungry for three miserable days and nights in our empty apartment in Anchorage before a kind man named Moses brings us to the Anchor Cattle Company in Homer, Alaska; offering us room and board for our honest labor. He has no idea what a chance he is taking on us. Or, maybe he does. Maybe Moses is an angel himself. I shudder to think what would have become of us if Moses had not taken that chance. Shane and I arrive in Homer lost, broken souls (me at the end of myself and

Shane in his element). Shane is living on the edge, the dangerously razor sharp edge of his survival instinct. You cannot get close to him and not get hurt.

We have been together for seven years (husband and wife for five) and I have lost myself in being his wife. The summer I turn eighteen, Shane and his handsome danger, blast into my life on a Harley-Davidson. Everything I think I know about life (good and bad) shatters; crumbles into a pile of dust, and is carried away by an early summer breeze before my 19th birthday. By the end of that first year there is no me left. It is a whirlwind year of grief, discovery and experimentation that leaves me lost, hollow and sharp around the edges. I don't think so much as react. All that matters is what Shane thinks and how Shane feels, whether or not Shane is happy, warm, satisfied and comfortable. My needs are secondary or non-existent. Much later I will learn that I enable him to treat me like this, that we live a sick co-dependent existence and that all my life I have never known any other way to be. We are not two people sharing our lives together, we are Shane living his life, and me helping him live it because that's all he can tolerate.

Everyone close to Shane is just another player in the drama of his life. He is off-the-charts smart, is handsome enough and has just enough charisma to draw you in with his crazy ideas. His words are loud, thought-provoking and right even when they're wrong. They swim through your brain leaving you breathless in their wake, wishing you could think that big.

We don't eat much that first year. We're trying to live off what Shane can earn at a real job making parts for airplanes. I'm going to business school to learn how to be an executive secretary. Mrs. Hawkins is teaching me shorthand. I practice on the weekends during the Dallas Cowboy's football games. I get up to 120 words per minute but cannot keep up with John Madden when he gets excited about another Hail Mary pass Roger Staubach throws and Golden Richards catches as the crowd goes wild. Shane sits on the edge of the sofa next to me, yelling at the television. He is shirtless. His lean, muscular chest and arms glisten with the sweat of this labor. He keeps the hand towel from the bathroom in his lap and occasionally mops up the sweat that drips down his sides. For three hours every week he yells at the TV screen, jumps up and down, hoots and hollers America's Team to their weekly victories.

We're lucky if we eat five or six meals all week; a burger and fries at the Pit Grill or a bowl of minute rice at home smothered with a can of Campbell's Chunky Soup can carry us for two days. I can cook rice and I can heat up a can of soup. I can scramble eggs too but Shane will only eat eggs if they're burnt, so I move his two eggs around in the skillet with the spatula over a high heat until they've been reduced to brown crumbles that pop around in the pan. When the smell starts to make me sick I know his eggs are just the way he likes them.

After his are done, I wash the pan out in the sink to cool it down and then cook mine over easy. Shane also likes fried bologna sandwiches with mustard and fried potatoes with ketchup.

Occasionally, when we have ten bucks, we make a trip to the Colonial Cafeteria for chicken-fried steak, mashed potatoes, gravy, a roll, and iced tea and we leave stuffed to the gills. I lose twenty pounds before the year is over and now I'm no bigger than a minute.

Shane and I are used to going a day without eating now and then, but not eating anything for three whole days before we get to the cattle ranch breaks something inside of me leaving a silent, ugly scar in its wake. You miss a meal and maybe you notice your tummy growling. You miss a day of eating and you feel your hunger. You miss three days of eating and your hunger takes on a life of its own. Your stomach is a big burning hole you cannot ignore and your brain turns to mush. You're hungry enough to beg, borrow and steal for a scrap of food. You look at shoe leather and cardboard and wonder what it would taste like, thinking if you could choke it down, at least there would be something in your stomach.

We have lost everything on our journey to Alaska and most of it I don't miss and will never think of again. I'm sorry I don't have my high school ring anymore and I'm upset about losing my mom's dining room table, chairs and china cabinet, but what I truly miss are my family and friends. Shane misses his gun and the money. He was down to one gun (his favorite) a Colt .45 Cold Cup with custom walnut laser-engraved grim-reaper grips. He had that gun for years, and is mourning it now like a lost loved one. I wonder if he would miss me as much if I were gone. He used his Gold Cup most recently to shoot his way out of an ambush led by an ambitious small-town Texas Sheriff and a handful of wide-eyed deputies. Now we are a long way from home with nothing left of our Texas lives. We are destitute, cold and hungry in our empty apartment in Anchorage and all Shane can do is rant and rave about not having that gun.

Shane is an avid gun collector and a quick-draw enthusiast. Over the years I have seen him practice for hours standing bare-chested in his bell-bottomed Levi's drawing two antique western revolvers from a gunslinger's holster, twirling them on his index fingers and sliding them back into their well-oiled slots. He is Clint Eastwood in a spaghetti western. He is fast. He is accurate. He will tell you that in a previous life he was a gun-slinging outlaw in the old west. His steely stare, his hazel eyes narrowed to slits and his wickedly sly grin will convince you he's telling the truth even if you don't believe in reincarnation. At one time he had over 100 guns: revolvers, rifles, shotguns, semi-automatics and automatics. He made me learn how to shoot them all for when the end of the world came and we would have to go underground to live. I even had my own Gold Cup and could take it apart and put it back together in seconds. We used to sit around and clean guns for fun. Before we left Texas he slept with a loaded .38 Special under his pillow because you never know when some crazy motherfucker will show up and try to kill you. His nightmares sometimes come even when he is awake. One crazy night, in a drug-induced stupor, he shot his .45 at me. The bullet whistled over my head and disappeared through the sheetrock leaving a black hole where there wasn't one before.

Now, here in our cold apartment, Shane is holding his right hand like it is a gun, the way little boys sometimes do when they're playing cops and robbers. His index finger is pointing at me. I am afraid that Shane has lost his mind, afraid of what I know he could do to me with his bare hands. He motions with his finger for me to step away from the front door of the apartment, to go sit down in the corner, and I obey. It is Sunday morning. We have been here for 48 hours without food and I am starving. I want to go dig through garbage, sweep floors, wash dishes, and do whatever anyone will let me do for some food. Shane wants to stay holed up in the apartment like the outlaw he is. He says the hunger will make us stronger.

We are waiting for Monday morning. Just 24 hours to go; waiting to see if Moses will keep his promise. It's a crapshoot. Will Moses come back and take us to the ranch he says he owns in Homer? He said we could work for room and board. Will he forget us like some forgotten shirt at the dry-cleaners? Will he call the police? Maybe he already has. Maybe the police will bust down the door any minute. We are both thinking these things but not speaking them. Putting words to our fears would give them too much power.

There is no furniture in our apartment. There is no food. There is nothing, not a single drinking glass, not a bar of soap, not even a roll of toilet paper. I lie curled in the fetal position on the cheap carpet like a broken piece of furniture someone has no use for. Shane paces back and forth, back and forth, talking his shit and flinging his index finger for emphasis. He is a marathon talker. He is a champion pacer. He's been known to wear out the carpet. Sometimes he lies down with me, my back against his front, his arms wrapped tight around me. I couldn't move even if I had the nerve. And I don't. I am incapable of doing anything to help myself. He is in control. It's always like that with him. You lose control in his presence. If you're not careful, you will lose yourself altogether like I have. The floor is hard, the room is cold and all I can feel is his hot breath in my ear, his ugly words reminding me of my place, my role in his life. My pathetic weaknesses.

I do not use profanity – most likely because my mom washed my mouth out with a bar of Dove soap when I was seven years old, and it left an impression. I had called my sister a shit-ass (one of the many colorful words I'd heard around the house) and mama overheard me. To this day I can't use Dove soap and profanity stings my ears. Shane, on the other hand, doesn't know how to talk without cuss words and when he gets started, he can hardly stop. Now is one of those times.

You goddamn people are so fucking weak. Run to your fucking mommy when life gets hard. Let me tell you about life, sweetheart. Life will chew you up and spit you the fuck out. Life will fucking kick you in the balls when you're not looking. Life's a bitch and then you die. You hear me? They won't get me, the sorry sons-of-bitches. I'll outsmart their stupid pansy asses. Ain't no hill for a stepper! Son of a bitch, are you crying again? You're fucking pathetic. Get the hell away from me with your fucking sniffling snot. Be a fucking soldier like I taught you. Don't let them fucking see you cry. Chin up! We're going to win this fucking war, baby. To hell with all those motherfuckers! You're not hungry. You don't know what in the goddamn hell hunger is. Be strong. Mind over matter, baby. You're old man has it. Fucking-A! I'm a tough son-of-a-bitch. Get out of my fucking face. Where are you going? Get your ass back over here. godammit! Motherfucker!

We are soldiers. Our hunger is a test. I am failing miserably.

When he sleeps, and if he sleeps long enough for the sting of his words to fade, there is wonderful silence in my head. I protect the puffy fullness of this blessed silence by bullying away my own loud thoughts. There are boxing gloves in my head. When words pop into my mind I punch them away with the boxing gloves before they can string together into sentences, sending them over the edge, keeping them out of my brain. My brain is wide open and I am Mohammad Ali boxing away my fears, my regrets; my life. If I'm lucky, this exercise makes me tired enough to fall asleep. When your sleep isn't riddled with the wicked nightmares of your sins, you can almost forget where you are, why you're there, and the burning hole of hunger in your stomach.

The drive from Anchorage to Homer feels much longer than the half a day it takes. This is due partly to my uncomfortable perch on Shane's bony lap, and partly to my state of weakness from not eating for three days. Our driver, Moses, keeps his promise and picks us up early Monday just like he said he would when he had dropped us off Friday morning. A warm place in my heart tells me that he wouldn't have left us there if he had known we were going to go hungry in a cold, empty apartment, waiting for him. But he came back for us and I am near tears with gratefulness.

The three of us are piled into the front seat of Moses' El Camino again. It is very cramped, but we are out of that apartment and on the road, a road that will hopefully lead to our next meal. Shane lied and said we had eaten breakfast when Moses asked us as we were getting into the car. In retaliation I am trying to hurt the tops of Shane's legs with my bony butt.

I steal quick glances at Moses, the man who holds our future in his hands. I hope he really is a good man and is not taking us into a situation even more dire than the one we have just left. Then I notice how he is holding the steering wheel; left hand palm up at seven o'clock, and right hand palm down at two o'clock; just like my dad drives. This is like a sign from an angel that I can relax and have faith that everything will be alright. Now I let my mind go wild and do not box away the words that come to me. I conjure up every admirable trait and positive characteristic I can think of and bestow them on Moses. Whether it is all true or not, I'll never know, but right then, I have to believe that

Moses is the best kind of man, the kind of man whose dogs love him so much they stay in the yard even when the gate is left open.

There is a lot of road construction that takes us on many detours through picturesque towns. We drive south on Highway 1 for about an hour to a town called Portage. Moses stops here so we can see a glacier. We get out and walk around. I reach down and touch the dirty ice at my feet. It is cold. I look up and see a wide wall of ice spilling toward me, frozen in time. It is the most magnificent deep turquoise color, somehow opaque and translucent at the same time; a chunk of another world plunked down to earth. It feels like someone has left the door open on a giant freezer and I rub my goose bumpy arms. The coldness surrounds me like breath, like the glacier is breathing through the hundreds of vertical rivulets time has carved into its turquoise side. It is an awesome sight and experience I cannot fully appreciate because of the hunger that by now is making me very weak. We return to the car and my goose bumps slowly fade. The road turns west toward Cooper's Landing and we drive through Sterling, Soldotna, on to Kenai and finally, Homer. I am amazed that the mountains still have snow on them. July in Alaska is a world away from July in Texas.

Moses buys us lunch in one of those towns along Highway 1. My hunger is a visible throbbing ache wrinkling my forehead and consuming my every thought when we finally stop. I am near tears at the happy way every flavor is bouncing around in my mouth. It is a struggle not to devour my Quarter-Pounder with cheese too quickly. My dad served twenty-one years in the Air Force and he had told me once that in boot camp they made them chew every bite of their food at least twenty times. I barely manage five or six chews before I'm swallowing and taking another huge bite. Shane sits next to me gobbling down his own cheeseburger and stuffing handfuls of hot, salty fries into his mouth. Moses sits across from us, on his own yellow plastic chair using manners. I wonder if he can tell how famished we are. If he can he doesn't let on. He is a nice man. I look around his smallish frame, out the plate-glass window of McDonalds and imagine the snow-capped mountains in the distance are blessing me, telling me it gets better from here on out.

Homer, Alaska is famous for its spit. Jutting four and a half miles into the Kachemak Bay, it is the world's longest landmass that Webster's defines as a narrow point of land extending into a body of water. I have never heard of a spit before. Moses drives us out to the end of the spit to show us the harbor where hundreds of charter and commercial fishing boats call home. Moses is proud of his state, his town, and I am happy to indulge him. Shane and I are getting our own private tour and it is so much easier to enjoy it now that we have eaten. Not being hungry makes me feel like somebody again.

Standing on the edge of the world famous Homer spit, considering the blur of events that has brought me here, I wonder who this person is that's living inside my skin. And I wonder what my family and friends in Texas must be thinking about me because it has been two weeks since I left home without a chance to say good-bye.

At the end of Bald Mountain Road, on the edge of a deep wooded area, Moses pulls the El Camino to a stop in front of a beautifully rustic log cabin.

We built it ourselves! Moses says with pride.

I look out the car window at the huge log walls and can't wrap my mind around the process that must have brought those trees here to rest one on top of another; silent, unmoving and horizontal. To the right of the cabin is a barn and I can see two horses; their heads down, tails swishing. As we unload from the car Moses points out the greenhouse, the Quonset hut (which he explains is his house when he stays here) the magnificent strawberry patch by the front porch and down the hill, the fifth-wheel trailer with a closed-in wooden porch built onto the front of it, a black stove pipe sticking out the top.

You two can have the fifth-wheel Moses says, nodding in that direction.

That'll be great! Shane says for the both of us.

I catch Shane's eye and he gives me a smile and a nod as if to say this is sweet.

Moses tells us that he comes to Homer to check on his ranch every couple of months and to bring supplies from the city. This time he drops off the supplies, checks on the cattle, stays the night in his Quonset hut and is gone early the next morning. Shane and I will never see Moses again.

Let's get this stuff inside, Moses says, picking up a box from the bed of the El Camino and handing it to Shane. Moses gently hands me a brown grocery sack. Before we step away from the car a small sandy-haired boy has appeared and is climbing up on to the back bumper.

Hey Curtis! Moses says with a smile in his eyes. The apples are over here. Moses points Curtis to the front of the bed.

How was the trip? A gravelly voice asks. I turn and see a man with a three-day (mostly gray) beard, and a pretty teenage girl with straight blond hair coming toward us. The girl's brown eyes lock with mine for an instant before she climbs into the back of the truck with Curtis. I give her a meek smile.

Hello Wayne. We had a little rain coming out of Fairbanks on Friday and some construction south of Anchorage, but smooth for the most part.

Wayne looks at Shane as he and Moses shake hands.

Wayne, this is Roy and his wife, Vanessa. They're going to help us out this summer. How 'bout we set them up in the fifth-wheel?

Sure thing, says Wayne, smiling.

We exchange hellos and handshakes, then a brief moment of awkward silence. Wayne's thin face is wrinkled into a smile that makes his eyes almost disappear, his cheeks squinch into two leathery ping pong balls, reminding me of Pop-eye the Sailor Man.

Wayne is my foreman here on the ranch, Moses says, breaking the silence. Takes real good care of things. He'll get you all settled a little later.

Let's get this stuff inside, Moses says again, heading up the porch steps. We all follow with our boxes and bags.

In the kitchen Wayne tells us this here is my daughter, Jillian (we call her Jill) and my son, Curtis. Jill is 14 and Curtis is 10.

Curtis gives us a quick, shy wave and heads back outside. Jill walks past us carrying the box of apples, one already clenched between her teeth, apple juice dripping off her chin. She takes the box to the back porch and comes back still chewing, the bitten apple in one hand, wiping her mouth with the other.

Hi. Jill and I say to each other between timid smiles.

Shane smiles big at Jill and says Hey baby! Lifting his chin slightly with confidence.

She briefly meets his gaze; smiles, blushes, and looks down at her bare feet sticking out from the bottom of her faded blue jeans. I follow her gaze and see worn pink polish on her toenails. I think to myself that it's too chilly to be barefoot.

Shane can't help flirting. Sometimes he flirts with the waitress at the Waffle House so much I wonder how well they really know each other. It's easy for me to see him in bed with any woman we come across because he makes no secret of his need to have more than one woman in his life. Even though I'm sick and tired of Shane, he is my husband and I get jealous at this little exchange between him and Jill. I stiffen at the thought of Shane in bed with this young, beautiful girl. I know already that it could happen.

When the truck is empty, Moses excuses himself and disappears into the Quonset hut.

The rest of us go back inside the log cabin. Just inside the door is a very large living space with a few pieces of old mismatched furniture and a huge fireplace against the far wall. The interior walls are the same as the exterior; long tree trunks laid horizontally with some type of mortar oozing between each one of them. I ask where the bathroom is and am pointed to the opposite side of the cabin from the kitchen. When I return to the kitchen, Shane is nowhere around. Wayne has just finished unpacking the contents of all the boxes and bags on the countertops and Jill has begun putting things away. There are 20 lb. bags of flour, sugar and corn meal; boxes of salt, jars of spices, crackers, yeast, peanut butter, canned goods, huge jugs of cooking oil, and other staples covering every flat surface. After going hungry all weekend I am in awe of all this food. I begin handing items to Jill and I pay attention to where she puts them. Wayne pours himself a cup of coffee from an old aluminum percolator sitting on the stove and takes a seat at the table.

I look at the percolator and have a flashback to my childhood. Mama had one just like it that sat on the back burner of our harvest gold stove in Michigan. I remember seeing my reflection in it when I was just knee-high to a grasshopper. The smell of fresh coffee brings me to the kitchen where mama is sitting at the yellow Formica table. She is on the phone smoking a cigarette and she waves a backhand in my direction, sending me back to the basement to watch Bozo the Clown on the black and white TV with my sisters.

Somewhere in all the unpacking Wayne asks me if I can cook. Before I can answer it becomes clear what he is thinking. Right away he begins showing me where things are kept and I am happy that I paid attention while helping Jill unload. Wayne shows me how to turn on the propane stove, then he explains the idiosyncrasies of the electric stove; shows me the different cuts of moose meat in the freezer near the back porch, and before anyone can say welcome to the Anchor Cattle Company, the angels and I are cooking our first supper together.

Chapter Two

It is difficult to comprehend all that has transpired in the one week since Shane and I landed at the Anchorage airport on a non-stop flight from Seattle; not to mention the longest five days of my life before that, watching the world go by through the dirty window of a Greyhound bus on our ride from Denver to Seattle. When we first arrive in Anchorage we stay up all night waiting for it to get dark. The locals had to explain to us Texans that Alaska in July knows no darkness. We are in the land of the midnight sun. We are exhausted but it is still light outside and that light tells our bodies to stay awake. Our small hotel room has a dirty, narrow window a foot from the ceiling running the length of one wall, letting the dusky light of the Alaskan summer night spill into the room. Finally one night we go to the store and buy a roll of aluminum foil; come back, and standing on the rickety desk chair, Shane covers the window, blocking out the light. The artificially induced darkness helps us finally get some much-needed sleep.

After a couple groggy days of sleeping, eating and barely speaking to each other, we leave the hotel and Shane announces that we will rent an apartment. This sudden proclamation gives me false hope at the prospect of a normal life. Ever since we left Texas we haven't actually talked about what we will do here in Alaska. When you're on the run you don't stop to think much. Besides, Shane is not my favorite person in the world right now and the less I have to talk to him, the better. We're both skittish and jittery like a couple of fireflies trapped in an old mayonnaise jar.

That very afternoon we find a large two bedroom, two-bath apartment in a quiet area on the edge of town that backs up to the woods. It is one of the nicest places Shane and I have ever lived but it reminds me of the apartment in Palmdale, California where Shane more or less abandoned me a few years back, and I get moody from the memories. Shane senses the change in me and I don't tell him what I'm thinking but he gets mad and yells about how I don't appreciate anything.

Moving in takes us less than a minute. All we have is one small duffle bag each. That's all we brought with us to start this new life. Shane's borrowed duffle bag is slightly larger and considerably heavier than mine because he has his Gold Cup in one of the outside zippered pockets. When he isn't carrying the bag, the gun is tucked neatly into his jeans at the small of his back. He is uncomfortable without a gun close by. I sometimes imagine the gun going off and blowing away one of his tiny butt cheeks but it never happens. He wears a black *Member's Only* jacket to conceal the butt of the gun, the sleeves of the jacket pushed up on his forearms like he's ready for action.

The rent for our new apartment is $600 per month. I gasp at this absurd amount but Shane doesn't bat an eye. We're a long way from the $250 a month duplex in Arlington, Texas where Shane lived when we first met. The Alaskan landlord requires a one-month deposit, the first month's rent and the last month's rent. Shane proudly hands over the cash (a pile of dirty but neat fifty and twenty dollar bills). I try not to worry about us using up all our money too fast. And later, when we end up only sleeping in that apartment a total of four nights, I want to get our deposit back from the landlord but Shane says no, that bridge is burned.

The other outside zippered pocket of Shane's duffel bag is stuffed with sealed white envelopes containing fifties, twenties, tens, fives, and the occasional one hundred dollar bill. Our whole world has been reduced to twenty-three thousand dollars cash. Enough money, Shane says, to give us a good start at a new life. The thoughts I keep to myself are that Shane only knows one way to be, one life to live, and no amount of money is going to change that. We will live the same life here that we've lived everywhere else and I am tired just thinking about it.

Shane is freakishly particular about his money; an obsession I'm certain is one of the many repercussions of his torturous childhood. Every bill has to be stacked face up with the heads of Benjamin Franklin, Ulysses S. Grant, Andrew Jackson, Alexander Hamilton and Abraham Lincoln all pointing to the right. There can be no dog-eared corners or unwanted folds. He spends hours straightening the corners, smoothing out the wrinkles, turning each bill the right way and counting them once, twice, three and four times. After all the bills are finally ready he separates them into groups of one thousand dollars and seals them in small white envelopes; the top flap of the envelope folded not at the crease but farther down at the top of where the stack of bills reaches. The finished product looks like a thick dollar-bill sized letter waiting for someone to address it, stick a stamp on it and put it in the mailbox. But he doesn't write anything on the envelopes. There's no need. Everyone in Shane's world knows that a sealed white dollar-billed size envelope means that a thousand dollars of neatly stacked bills is tucked inside. Shane is very generous with these tidy white envelopes. I've lost count of how many envelopes he has given away to friends and acquaintances. He tosses them into open hands still sealed like they are candy with little or no concern of being paid back. It doesn't matter why the money is needed -- bills, food, a business venture -- Shane often doesn't even want to know. He has a big place in his heart for people who need his money.

We can't get the heater to come on in our new apartment. And as the outside temperature dips into the 40s I think we are going to freeze to death lying on the floor with no covers. I pull on one t-shirt after another; everything in my bag that I can layer on, but still my teeth are chattering, my nose running. The heating unit is located in the hallway and late that first night Shane spends some time banging around on it until a neighbor pokes an angry head out his adjacent door. The neighbor doesn't say anything or offer to help. He just gives Shane a look that says you're crazy for wanting the heat on in July.

When Shane comes back and tells me we have an angry neighbor across the hall I am reminded of other angry neighbors from our past. We had just moved into an apartment in

Fort Worth, from a ratty old farm house in Cleburne, and we made enemies of all our neighbors that first night by flooding our apartment and the one next door with an exploding waterbed mattress.

Shane's cousin, Robert, helps us move from Cleburne and then Shane has to take him back home around midnight when we're finally finished. Shane and Robert set up the king-size waterbed when we first get to the apartment and it has been filling up for a couple of hours. Before they leave Shane says he's turned off the water, but instead of turning it off he has mistakenly turned it on full blast.

I am exhausted and have to go to work the next day so as soon as they leave I crash on the couch; all our belongings still in boxes stacked around on the floor of the one bedroom apartment that suddenly seems way too small.

Sometime later, when I'm deep in sleep and dead to the world, I am brought wide awake by a very loud BOOM! It sounds like a shotgun blast at close range. I jump up off the couch and am standing in two inches of very cold water. The water seems to be coming from the bedroom and I run around the corner into the room and flick on the overhead light. It is a disaster. The waterbed frame has given way under the pressure of the overfilled mattress and one of the sideboards has gone through the wall into the apartment next door. Through a hole the size of a large watermelon, a river of water is escaping into the darkness of that apartment. The curtains have been ripped from the window and are sloshing around in the water at the head of the bed. My heart is racing and I panic. I think to myself I must not let any more water escape from the torn mattress, that there has been too much damage already so I climb on to the bed and kneeling in the middle of the platform, I reach over and grab one corner of the rubbery mattress. With one corner in my grip I crawl over to the other side, the front of my t-shirt dragging in the cold puddle of water, and I try to grab another corner but the weight of the water still trapped in what's left of the mattress is too much, too heavy and I can't move it but I pull with all my might and struggle and struggle and eventually lose my grip on the one corner and have to start all over again. I grab, I pull, I crawl, I struggle, I lose my grip. Over and over again. I am exhausted and terrified but I can't stop grabbing, pulling, struggling. My brain won't let go of this idea that I have to prevent more water from escaping. I am incapable of talking myself out of the craziness because I don't even realize that what I'm doing is crazy. I only know that I cannot let more water escape. I am drenched from head to toe, my lips are turning blue, my teeth are chattering; my nipples are straining against the wet t-shirt clinging to my body. My bare arms and legs are covered in goose bumps but I keep up my struggle. Then there is a tap, tap, tap, on the bedroom window. Startled out of my private nightmare I look up and see three wide-eyed strangers (a guy and two girls) staring at me in disbelief through the glass. I stare blankly back at them. The guy is talking to me.

Are you ok? What happened?

I don't respond, I'm just staring at them staring at me. Then the guy starts pointing to the front door and yelling at me to open the door so they can come in and help. It takes me a few seconds to register what he is saying and even longer to give up my grip on the mattress.

When Shane comes home asking what the fuck, the maintenance man has been running the water vacuum for over an hour, mumbling and grumbling under his breath; the cheap carpet going bald in huge clumps. The lady from next door, whose closet is now flooded, stays long enough to bitch me out about all her ruined clothes and shoes then leaves in her car, tires squealing. The couple from upstairs is quietly helpful for a while. They were glad to learn that the big boom hadn't been a gunshot. After I open the front door for them and everyone discovers what the problem is, he goes back to their apartment and brings back two brooms. Together they sweep water out the doors, him out the front door and her out the back patio, until the maintenance man comes. Then they leave with their brooms, quietly wishing me luck, careful not to look around at the devastation they are leaving me with. I watch them leave wondering what their names are and why they have two brooms. I never see them again.

It's years before we can laugh about that night. We believe that the swollen waterbed mattress had probably almost filled the room before its seam gave way. We had seen this happen before. A guy named Tom who lived next door to us in the duplex in Arlington got a waterbed one day; started filling it, forgot about it, went to the store and returned hours later. He turned off the water and came pounding on our door. Come see! Come see! The top of his new king-size waterbed mattress was about a foot from touching the ceiling. It was one giant blue water balloon perched on the wood frame that seemed insanely tiny and it scared the crap out of all of us. We just knew that any second it would blow and we'd all die in what would be described on the evening news as the great waterbed tidal wave. Tom started it draining into the backyard then came and sat in our living room with us. We all got high and spent the evening talking and laughing about how much water that thing could hold.

So now we're in Alaska, in another new apartment and already we've made our closest neighbor mad at us. Normally when someone gives Shane any shit he's in their face but this time he apologizes for the noise and quickly retreats back into the apartment, giving up on the heater. We can't afford to call any attention to ourselves.

The next day Shane announces that it's time to go shopping. We both agree that the first thing we need to buy is a vehicle so we grab a newspaper from the corner store and walk a few blocks to a restaurant for breakfast. While we walk I imagine us buying groceries, a couch, a bed and lots of blankets after we get a car but we don't end up buying a single thing on my list that day. Sitting in a booth eating pancakes because they're cheap, Shane circles several prospects. Back in Texas we had owned a very nice black Chevy Blazer that Shane had spent way too much money on adding a four inch lift kit, oversized tires, chrome running boards, fog lights and a 1000 lb. electric winch that rescued us from countless ditches and muddy creek bottoms. Shane knows we probably won't find anything as nice as our old truck but he's hoping to find another Blazer. There are only two listed. We get some quarters and Shane calls the two people selling their Blazers. One sounds good and one has been wrecked. Reluctantly Shane circles ads for a Jeep and several Fords even though he hates a Ford like the plague. He makes several more calls and narrows the list. Soon it is time to call a taxi. Shane shows our driver the list of addresses and after a few minutes the driver has mapped out a plan of attack and off we go.

Our bearded driver looks and smells like he lives in this car. The front seat is littered with a mountain of clothing and assorted papers and garbage. Riding in the back seat, with the windows down for fresh air, I clutch my leather shoulder bag full of tidy white envelopes and Shane holds on to our marked-up copy of the classifieds. It is late in the afternoon when we finally find our truck.

To pay for the late model red Ford Bronco we follow the seller into a faded singlewide trailer with no under-skirting and a graduated stack of cinderblocks for stairs. Inside, he leads us to the kitchen table and pushes a half-eaten plate of food aside. I open four envelopes, count out $3,300 and lay it on the table beside a bowl of dried macaroni and cheese. The family whose dinner we have interrupted is silently sitting in the darkening living room watching a TV that has been muted. The dad picks up the pile of money and slides it into the front pocket of his worn jeans. I see that every fingernail on each hand is outlined in black grease and the wrinkles in his knuckles are filled with the same black grime. I think to myself hadn't he washed those hands before eating supper? My eyes, needing something else to look at, dart away. They land on the dirty floor and I begin counting the harvest gold diamonds that connect the corners of the 12" linoleum squares. Seventeen across plus nine to the refrigerator and nine back again. Shane and the mechanic are talking about the truck. As I'm counting to seventeen in my mind I catch some of their words and my mind latches on to them randomly the way it always wants to do; forcing me to spell them over and over again: Gas mileage m-i-l-e-a-g-e, m-i-l-e-a-g-e; two owners o-w-n-e-r-s; new tires, t-i-r-e-s, t-i-r-e-s, t-i-r-e-s. Then my eyes look back at the table t-a-b-l-e. Four chairs at the table, sixteen legs, four edges to the table, 1, 2, 3, 4, 1, 2, 3, 4, 1, 2, 3, 4. A picture hangs crooked on the wall; it has four sides, 1,2,3,4,1,2,3,4. My eyes bounce back to the mechanic as he pulls the truck title from his back pocket and signs his name. I hold my breath. Shane takes the title, shakes the dirty right hand of the seller and we walk out the door; me counting the steps back to the truck and spelling d-i-r-t-y over and over again in my head. Shane pays the taxi driver and sends him on his way. We are miles down the road before I relax enough to just count the white lines as they speed past. Before I know it, I'm on 187 and I don't remember getting there. I am exhausted as I let out a breath it feels like I've been holding for hours.

It feels good to have our own wheels even if it is a Ford. We head downtown to an Army/Navy store the taxi driver told us about and we buy some Alaska stuff; sleeping bags, green army blankets, sweaters, gloves, pants, long underwear, and a jacket for each of us. Across the street is a Red Wing shoe store where we each get new boots. Walking out of that store, I'm not sure where my new western-style work boots will take me, but I like the way they look and feel on my feet. I've never worn boots like these. They make me feel strong, tall and invincible. These boots are substantial. They evoke power and confidence. With boots like these, good things could happen. Shane gets some cool boots too but I like mine better. We both pay extra for thick wool insoles and stroll out of the store wearing them; my Levis 501s tucked into the tops of mine. Back in the truck I ask about finding a grocery store to stock the kitchen of our new apartment before we head home but Shane just says no, it's time to hit the road.

We're gonna explore the last frontier, baby!

He reaches over and grabs my left knee, giving it a squeeze that he knows tickles me like crazy and I jump and let out a playful squeal for his benefit. He says we can grab a cheeseburger somewhere if I'm hungry. I don't respond but he doesn't notice because he's already lost in the last frontier. Looking down at my new boots, I wonder if we're ever going to make it back to our expensive apartment again.

Shane had worked on the Alaskan pipeline when he was younger and ever since those wild and wonderful days he has talked about wanting to go back to the last frontier and live off the land. Early in our marriage I remember thinking that the simple life he described sounded romantic, exotic, and fun. But this is late in our marriage. Way late.

And the silent dread within me is growing bigger with each breath, each mile separating us from our new home. I'm careful not to let him see my worry, my disappointment so I turn and watch Anchorage slip away outside my window.

Shane's anger comes at me fast and violent like razor blades and shards of glass, cutting away parts of me with each vicious word. Over the years I have learned how to navigate my way in the wake of his wrath. My first line of defense is not to make him mad. Unsolicited questions from me often incite his rage so I don't ask about our empty apartment waiting in cold silence for our return.

We drive 372 miles north on AK-3 to Fairbanks because someone told us it was eighty degrees up there. So far in Anchorage the thermometer has not even reached seventy. For a couple of Texans (Shane native, me transplanted) our bones ache for the kind of rippling heat you can see dancing near the hot surface of the asphalt.

Somewhere along the mountainous highway, after we sleep for a couple of hours at a rest stop, Shane picks up a hitchhiker despite my brave pleas against it.

Chapter Three

The drifter and Shane exchange fake names and after looking through him for a second or two I turn my attention back to the countryside outside my window. With a southern accent the guy says he's from Tennessee. I don't like his long, greasy dishwater blond hair, his cold dark eyes, his large biceps, or his quiet, guilty manner. My mind races through one bad scenario after another wondering what brought him to the side of the road between Anchorage and Fairbanks, Alaska. I think to myself that he has surely committed far greater crimes than those that have landed me and Shane here. He doesn't talk much and I'm convinced that what little he does say must all be lies. I catch him staring at me once or twice and it makes me nervous.

Shane is calling himself Roy. It is hard for me to call him that but I have no choice. In my mind he does not look like a Roy. He should have let me pick the name I was going to have to call him. Chase would have worked because he is on the run, or Mark or Steve or anything but Roy. But he didn't ask me. He just makes me call him Roy, which ironically, means king -- another reason for me to hate calling him that. When you've been with a man named Shane for seven years it is not easy to suddenly start calling him Roy, but I do it, and I'm proud of myself for not slipping up so far. I don't get to pick an alias for myself. I think I would like to have been called Grace for a while, but Shane knows he would slip up, so he doesn't even try. I am still Vanessa, but only a wrung-out, tired version of myself.

There isn't much talking as we drive north through the middle of the night, the Alaskan summer night that doesn't grow dark. It just grabs on to the smudgy end of the daylight and holds it like a blanket until morning when the sun burns it away and the world is bright again. I am content to sit quietly, lost in the tangled web of regret playing over and over in my mind as I count the white lines. Counting and spelling has saved me all my life. It has kept me from thinking about the bad things, kept me from feeling the pain. The constant string of words or numbers form a wall of defense in my mind. Sometimes I have two walls going at the same time; one is a string of words, and one is a string of numbers and they are constantly looping in and out of each other. And now, counting the white lines is all that keeps me from slipping over the edge into the comforting bliss of billowy darkness that beckons me with more and more insistence. I can taste the darkness, feel the promise of sweet release, but the counting and the spelling keep me engaged, keep me just far enough from the edge that I don't fall into that place where nothing could ever touch me again.

I am furious at Roy for picking up Mr. Tennessee but part of me understands that Shane is a hustler who hasn't had anyone new to hustle in too many days, and another part of me is thankful to have another player to help me help Shane live his life, even if the new player might be an Tennessee ax murderer.

After hours on the road I feel thick and fuzzy. At some point I am relegated to the backseat so

Shane and Mr. Tennessee can talk easier. I lie down and drift in and out of a fitful sleep where I'm dreaming that I'm dreaming and the road turns into a river and I'm drowning, then I'm on a roller coaster and my screams are caught in my throat and now the roller coaster is an airplane and we will surely crash.

The three of us eat cheeseburgers at a picnic table in the 80° Fairbanks sunshine sometime the next day. When you don't have a clock or wear a watch and it doesn't get dark, it's impossible to know what time it is. There is no routine to help keep you grounded. No time clock to punch. No dinner to cook. No alarm clock to ring. There is just a nagging feeling of impending doom as the hours come and go unnoticed.

We drive around town all day. From my backseat perch it disappoints me to see that Fairbanks looks like just any other city. These people don't look any different than people anywhere else I've been. When you say you're from Texas people ask if you live on a ranch and ride a horse to work. They expect you to say yes. I am in northern Alaska and I expect to see Eskimos and igloos. These are just normal people with alarm clocks on their nightstands, milk cartons in their refrigerators and clothes in their closets; moving through their days, driving Fords and Chevrolets and living lives that I know are better than mine, safer than mine; normal.

This unstructured life is exhausting. The empty days hang on my shoulders heavy and hard. I am smothering under the weight of nothingness. It feels like I'm being sucked down the drain. Down, down, down, spiraling out of control and there is nothing to grab on to, nothing to stop the downward spiral. The counting and spelling barely help. What's left of my life is a living nightmare. I am so tired. Tired of riding in the backseat of the Bronco. Tired of feeling sick to my stomach. Tired of the incessant itching from my nervous rash. Tired of Shane's voice and all his lies. Tired of having Mr. Tennessee, the ax murderer with us. Tired of it always being light. Tired of trying to remember to call Shane Roy, and tired of being afraid that at any moment someone might recognize us from America's Most Wanted or from our photos that I imagine are surely on display in every post office across the country by now.

At least the rash isn't as bad as it had been on the five-day bus ride. Now it is only on the parts of my body I can cover with clothes. I've had some form of this rash all my life. Usually the rash is only on my arms and sometimes on my fingers. But when Shane showed up at my sister's apartment and took me away almost two weeks ago, the big blistery, itchy splotches from my childhood began popping up and eventually covered almost every inch of my body.

At one bus stop on the ride from Denver to Seattle (before we fly to Anchorage) we find a pharmacy. I go back to the counter where you pick up your prescriptions and ask the pharmacist if there is anything that will stop the itching. He looks at me like I have the plague. He actually takes a step backward, his face twisted in an ugly grimace as he points down an aisle saying something about Benadryl. I buy five kinds of creams, lotions and pills, but what works best is the spray. That way I don't have to touch my skin putting it on, because touching makes the itching worse and the itching is unbearable. Shane buys several bottles of Tylenol PM.

Mr. Tennessee is behind the wheel of the Bronco! I wake up from another bad dream and it is the back of his head I see on the driver's side, not Shane's and I am outraged. Shane is curled up in the passenger seat, sawing logs. I shoot darts at the back of both their heads with my incredulous eyes. What in the world is he thinking, letting an ax murderer drive us around while we both sleep? We have almost $20,000 cash in a bag here, not to mention my jewelry. I've caught Mr. Tennessee eyeing my 2 carat diamond pendant more than once, so I've taken it off and hidden it in the inside zipper pocket of my bag. There is no way I can go back to sleep now with this new anger inside me. One more bullet in the arsenal of anger tools I have been collecting; the tools that chisel away at what's left of mine and Shane's relationship.

Shane soon wakes up, seemingly refreshed. He and Mr. Tennessee start talking and laughing like a couple of old Army buddies sharing a beer at a neighborhood bar. I can't believe how Shane is opening up to this guy. He's telling him too much. Careful, I say over and over in my mind, hoping Shane will intercept my silent warnings. But it doesn't work and he just keeps talking. He's always been like that. He doesn't catch on to things normal people perceive. He's oblivious to other people's stares. Now he's either trying to gain Mr. Tennessee's confidence, or he has totally lost his mind because he practically tells our whole story.   More anger bullets for my arsenal.

We are on our way back to Anchorage now, somewhere south of Fairbanks in the middle of some of God's most gorgeous country. I am mad, tired, confused, and I need to pee.

It's not long before we pull off the highway. The rest stop is on the left side of the highway, up on a hill, with a little outcropping overlooking the road like a scenic turnout.   There are no other cars around – probably because it's most likely three o'clock in the morning.   I jump out of the Bronco and head to the ladies room. Shane gets out and stretches.

Nothing could have prepared me for what happens next.

I come out of the ladies room at exactly the same time Shane is walking out of the men's room. Walking toward each other, our eyes lock and we stop dead in our tracks. We look over to where the Bronco had been parked, look back at each other and then run to the scenic turnout. Desperately, our eyes search the highway; first north, then south, and together we catch a glimpse of the Bronco's red tailgate as it disappears over the horizon.

HE'LL COME BACK, I scream.   It's just a joke. He's gonna turn around and come back for us. HE HAS TO COME BACK. He wouldn't just leave us here on the side of the road. . . WOULD HE???!!!

My fists are full of the front of Shane's shirt. I am pulling and twisting, barely able to stand, barely able to breathe. Then my eyes meet his and I know. In a split second, my mind bends, expands, turns a new corner, makes a quantum leap, and finally acknowledges the dire truth. Mr. Tennessee is not coming back for us. This is not a joke. This is real. This is bad.

No! No! No! No! No!!! I scream; pushing Shane away so hard he stumbles backwards and almost falls.

Time stands still. My life flashes before my eyes like I've heard people describe when talking about a near death experience. Nothing makes sense. I am in shock. This is too huge, too much to add on top of everything else that has happened. My mind knows it is true but the rest of me is not ready to accept being stranded on the side of the road outside Fairbanks, Alaska with nothing but the clothes we are wearing. Shane has already processed the truth and moved on. His tough mind has gone straight to pick up and walk away.

Let's go, he says. There's nothing left for us here. And he starts walking.

But my legs won't move. Shock waves are coursing through my body. There is a loud non-noise in my head. I think I'm screaming but I can't hear anything. Shane comes back for me and puts an arm around my shoulder. His touch jolts me like lightning.

My denial turns to disbelief and then quickly to anger. I begin to pound on his chest and slap at his face and arms. I am releasing the full arsenal that has accumulated inside of me; every bullet of anger I have been collecting for seven years. He manages to grab my wrists and yells one profanity after another into my face, trying to force me to accept the truth. I wrestle from his grasp, push him away again and let go of my own angry words. I don't even know what I'm saying. I only know that it's over. This is the bottom. There is nothing left. A weird sense of freedom I've never known fuels my unleashed anger. I am not even worried that I might make him mad. What more can his anger do to me? I am already at the end of myself. And this anger is mine. It belongs to me. I have earned it. Now there is only the letting go, the cleansing release. My life is over. There is nothing left. I want to lie down and die right here on the gravel parking lot of the rest stop. The truck is gone. All of our Alaska clothes, my jewelry, all of the money. How will I ever get back to Texas? My only hope has just been driven away by a Tennessee thief in the middle of an Alaskan summer night.

At the end of my anger and bitter words, there is nothing. I stand empty and stunned on the outcropping looking south for a long time, tears dripping down on my new boots with the thick wool insoles. Shane stands quietly a few feet away from me.

Then we are walking. My feet are moving me forward. I cannot do it on my own. I cannot think beyond my next step. I cannot see past the toes of my own boots.

No words find their way between us, we just keep walking. No words even exist that can fill the void. An ocean of pain, fear and resentment is now wedged between us. It is a tangible, solid mass of hurt and I grab on to it for dear life. Holding on to the hot edge of it for comfort, for safety, it is the only real thing left in my life. It is the buoy that keeps me afloat, keeps me from drowning into the dark abyss of loss and despair. I am empty but for the hot anger pushing me down the road.

Chapter Four

There are not many cars traveling south on AK-3 in the middle of the night but each time a car passes Shane turns around and sticks out his thumb. I just stop and look at my boots. What must the mothers and fathers, brothers and sisters in those cars think of us as they drive by without stopping? I know how mad I was at Shane for picking up Mr. Tennessee and I don't blame them for driving on.

Moses, in his El Camino, is the only one who stops. He is traveling alone and looks to be in his mid-fifties. He is soft spoken and has kind, blue eyes the color of a good summer sky. I can just tell he's not an ax murderer. Through the lowered passenger side window he asks us where we're headed. Shane says Anchorage. With no other questions, Moses motions for us to hop in the back. We ride in the back of the El Camino for twenty or thirty minutes and then a light rain begins to fall from the sky that refuses to get dark. I decide that if Moses leaves us out here to freeze, maybe he isn't as nice a man as I had first decided. The rain picks up and we are getting wetter and wetter and I'm covered with a gazillion goose bumps. I think there is no way I'm going to make it all the way to Anchorage like this. It's too hard. Life is just too hard when all you are is a ball of drowning, freezing anger. I close my eyes and drop my head between my knees and let the cool raindrops slide down the back of my neck. Soon Moses stops the car and hollers for us to get in. He's a nice man again. Shane slides into the passenger seat and I climb onto his soggy lap, facing Moses. This is definitely better than being out in the rain but I sure wish Moses hadn't let us get so wet.

We ride like that all the way to our expensive apartment that we haven't seen in almost three days; the cold, empty apartment with no food, no furniture, no heat. It is the last place I want to go. It is the only place we can go.

Shane does all the talking. He tells Moses a watered-down version of how we ended up stranded. When Shane gets to the part about our truck and all our possessions being stolen, Moses wants to take us straight to the police to file a report. Shane convinces him to let us handle our own business.

Ain't nothin but a thang! Shane says.

Moses lets it go. If he thinks it's suspicious that we aren't in a hurry to go to the authorities, he never lets on. He continues to listen quietly and asks very few questions. I notice that Moses holds the steering wheel just like my father did. Now I like Moses more than ever.

Shane keeps on talking. He tells Moses that we've only been in Alaska for a few days. We rented a nice apartment in Anchorage. Just arrived from Tennessee (did I hear that right?). I am a secretary looking for a job. Shane is a private pilot looking to start a bush pilot service.

We'll be fine. Ain't no hill for a stepper.

His stories dance in and through, but mostly around the truth. His left hand has a loose grip on my left upper arm, and his right hand rests heavily on my right thigh. Each time his mouth tells a lie, his hands get heavier on me and I feel like a June bug stuck in a spider's web. I am tired. I am lost. I am in a stupor. It feels like my brain is dragging behind and Shane's new lies are just bouncing around outside of me. I find solace in watching the rain drops on the windshield. I am one of those rain drops and each time the wipers come, I am gone. Then I'm back. Now I'm gone. Then I'm back. Now I'm gone.

Then Moses is talking. He tells us about his cattle ranch in Homer. The name Homer sounds funny to me, like the name you would give a pet cow and I let out a small giggle. Moses smiles at my giggle and says he is on his way there but is stopping for the weekend to take care of some business in Anchorage. He asks if we might be interested in going to his ranch with him. He could pick us up on his way out of town early Monday morning. He can't pay us but offers room and board. Says he always needs extra help in the summer.

Moses drops us off at our apartment around 8:00 a.m. Friday morning. We agree to be ready Monday morning to head to Homer. Shane and I let ourselves into the empty apartment and crash on the floor, Shane wrapped around me for warmth because now we don't have extra clothes we can layer on.

Later that day I open my eyes. Shane is still sleeping behind me. I am weak and hungry and homesick and tired. I cannot see how we will survive until Monday morning waiting for Moses to come back.

I begin to cry. First tears stream silently down my cheeks but soon I am sobbing uncontrollably. I cry for my lost life in Texas. I cry for what's been lost in Alaska. I cry for knowing I married the wrong man. I cry because

I am homesick and desperately want to talk to my family. I cry at the mess I've made of my life. I cry because I am lost. I am lost physically, emotionally, and spiritually. I am weak and sad and pathetic and lost and I just want to go home.

Shane wakes up and tells me to shut the fuck up. But I can't stop. He goes into the bathroom and closes the door in disgust. When he returns the tears have finally dried up and I am curled into a fetal position. A low, rhythmic moan is seeping from somewhere deep within me.

Shane doesn't speak. He paces the floor in a circle around me. Long stretches of time pass.

Later, he is ready to talk again and his words fly at me sharp and mean. My grief is too heavy for his shoulders. He has taken my pain and molded it between his strong, lean fingers; twisted the validity of my grief into words he can live with, and now throws them into my face as disgust and shame.

That's it, that's enough. Son-of-a-bitch! Get up off the floor. godammit! He grabs my arm and pulls me until I'm standing and now I'm crying again. Motherfucker! Stop crying. It's time for you to be a fucking soldier. This is the real motherfucking thing. It's you and me baby. We're in this together. This is what I've been training you for. We need to be strong. It's mind over matter. Run in place with me. Then we'll do some push-ups. We gotta be strong. We're going to win this motherfucking war, godammit!

So we jog in place until we're both sweating and then we do push-ups until I collapse and sleep some more.

I know part of what it is that makes Shane get this way, but knowing doesn't make it any easier to love him.

Shane was raised in east Texas by his maternal grandmother until he was six years old. His mother had given birth to him and then checked herself out of the hospital, leaving baby Shane there. His grandmother went and got him, loved him, fed him, nurtured him and sent him to school. He was a bright, thriving, six-year old boy with almond-shaped hazel eyes, an easy smile, blond hair and a heart of gold when his mother came back to claim him. His little world shattered that day. Shane's mother took him from the only home he had ever known, into a world of uncertainty, poverty, and a string of abusive stepfathers. With each new stepfather, there was a new baby. Shane loved his brothers and sisters and pretty much raised them himself as they moved from one ramshackle rent house to another. When he was fourteen, something happened that would change his life forever. Shane shot his stepfather for doing something unthinkable to one of his baby sisters, then threw down the gun and ran half way across Texas. He would learn years later that he had not killed the man.

Shane lived on the streets of Dallas and surrounding areas for years, in and out of foster homes and juvenile detention centers, and later jails and prisons. He dropped out of school in 10th grade. Later, he got his GED, took some college courses and taught himself how to fly an airplane. He got his pilot's license a few months after we met.

Shane is a lanky, wiry man. He is 5'11" but likes to say he's six feet tall. At his heaviest, he barely weighs 150 pounds. His long legs are skinny, but his chest is full, and he's got thin but muscular arms. I've seen much bigger men cower down in fear of Shane, unwilling to test his wiry strength. Not many people get close to Shane, but there are a small handful of us who know that the broken heart of a six-year-old boy is hiding beneath the tough, leathery exterior he shows the world.

Whenever Shane launches into one of his screaming tirades I try to picture that sweet, innocent six-year old boy trying to understand the cruel world, and when I catch a glimpse of him I know everything will be ok. But no matter how hard I try I cannot find that tenderhearted little boy in Shane now. Maybe I am too wrapped up in my own dark misery to see it. Maybe that little boy isn't there anymore. Maybe the scared little girl in me won't let anything else in; keeping it all on the other side of the walls she built around her heart so many years ago.

A child's heart can only absorb so much hurt before she learns to build walls for protection. One wall goes up to absorb the yelling and screaming, another to block the sight of her parents hitting each other. Still more walls to hide all the secrets and shame, to disguise the fear, keep people at a distance; the walls forming a maze she gets lost in each morning when another day comes; another day of hiding behind walls, of not letting herself be disappointed.

Time crawls while we wait for Moses to return. Shane won't let me leave the apartment, even to find food, so I give up and try to sleep.

After a while I can't tell if I am awake or dreaming. I am lost in a maze of random memories. I can't see a future, it's all about the past, all about emotions and feelings and it makes me tired and hopeless. All the hope that Moses had given me by offering us room and board has disappeared; it grew claws and fangs, devoured itself and now it haunts me in the cold light of day; mocking me and my feeble hope of getting out of this mess alive. As sure as I am that we will never see Mr. Tennessee again, I am now positive that Moses is also gone for good.

Hunger has a way of sucking the life out of you, eating holes in your memories and gobbling up any thoughts you try to form of a future, leaving you lost in the naked void of nothingness. A pathetic, moaning blob curled into a fetal position on the floor. As the hours crawl by, I slip further and further into the private hell inside my head.

Simultaneously, I pray for Moses to return, and expect him not to. It's a trick I learned as a child. It is so much easier to expect the worst than to hope for the best and be disappointed.

You never know what you can endure until you've lived through it and you hear yourself telling the story to someone years later.

Shane and Vanessa, circa 1983

Chapter Five

Once you have smelled the stink that comes from cooking methamphetamine, you never forget it. You can't forget it. If it had a face, the noxious stench would surely be a cousin to the Gorgon. Still living on the edge of the world, but unlike Medusa and her sisters who turned their onlookers into stone, the Meth Monster turns its users into skeletal strung-out junkies who stay up for days lying, cheating and stealing to get their next fix. Imagine the stench of a human body that hasn't washed for fifty years. Bottle that stench and stir in two or three noxious chemicals. Cook it over a high heat for 24 hours and you're getting close to the stink of methamphetamine. You catch a whiff of the stink years later driving through a neighborhood and you know there's a meth lab somewhere close. If you get near the stink, it makes its way into your body, assaults your every sense, and takes up residence under your skin. Only the passing of time will eradicate it; and it can take weeks. While you wait, the stink steadily seeps out through your pores like the monster it is and contaminates everything you touch.

Shane gets the recipe for crank (handwritten on several pages of notebook paper) as payment for a drug deal and brings home the stink many times. I wash his clothes three times in a row and they begin to take on the Tide fresh scent, but now the washing machine has the stink. The chair he sits in for dinner gets the stink. Every pore in his body oozes the stink, and weeks later I still smell it in his sweat. It contaminates everything he touches. It contaminates me. The couch, the bed, the doorknobs, they all get the stink. You can smell it from the front porch before you knock on our door.

I worry when I go to the store that people can smell it on me. Paranoia has me convinced that everyone is staring, pointing; blaming me for the awful smell I've dragged in. I am Pigpen and I take my smell with me wherever I go. So I stop going places. I stay home where the stink burns away my sense of smell while I wait for it to pass.

The year is 1984. George Orwell warned us about Big Brother and the Thought Police, and both are alive and very real in the mind of my husband. He believes he is being watched, listened to. I think maybe he is right, maybe the police are tapping our phone line or watching our house but what I don't know yet is that Shane thinks "they" have implanted a listening device into his brain and that his thoughts are being intercepted. He thinks that "they" use radio waves in an attempt to control him. He thinks he can outsmart them by thinking one thing and believing another. It will be a few years before I hear Shane speak these scary secrets of his. For now I just think the meth he is cooking at some remote location, and bringing home to sell, is making him more paranoid than usual. He is very intense. He is redefining intensity. He is so intense that sometimes I wonder if he is from another planet. He sees things differently than normal people. He looks through a thought and attacks it from the other side just in case it is a trick. His mind wraps around a simple thought and squeezes it until one brilliant pearl of an idea, shiny and polished escapes his lips. I watch quietly from my corner of the couch, my seat in the car, my side of the bed and I decide that he is wired too tight, that something has got to give. He thinks too much. He is convinced that only he can save the world. He stays up for days thinking. I watch him swallow a handful of Valium and it only brings him down a couple of notches. He still does not sleep. He smokes one joint after another and it doesn't seem to faze him. The cavern developing between us grows in direct proportion to his increasing intensity.

Several times, through the years, being with Shane wears me down and I have to get away. His harsh words get stuck inside my head and begin to make me crazy so I take a suitcase, fill it with a few changes of clothes, and drive. Friends and family are always there for me with an extra bed or living-room couch for a few days. Once, I fly all the way to Florida and stay with my mom and her current husband and am actually gone for a few weeks. But current husband is mean, homesickness sets in, Shane says all the right things on the telephone and I go back. I go back because my life with Shane is all I know. He has twisted himself into my wounded mind, wedged his broken self into the folds of my own broken heart. I have melded my life around him and don't know how to function when he is not there torturing me with his sad, hard love. Vulnerable, confused and weak I'm drawn back into the folds of Shane's sick comfort. He welcomes me, holds me, strokes me, tells me he loves me, touches me gently, whispers into my ear how much he missed me and that he doesn't ever want to spend another night without me and we sleep soundly tangled in the sheets of our blissful lovemaking. I am home.

The next day I'm folding laundry in the bedroom and hear Shane yell at me from his perch on the couch in the living room. Woman, I need some iced tea. There is a pitcher of tea in the refrigerator that I made earlier and he knows it is there but I am the woman. I must stop what I'm doing, get a glass, fill it with ice, pour the tea and take it to him. Don't let it fucking get empty! He snaps as I place the glass on the coffee table in front of him, careful not to block his view of the television. I am home. There's nothing sadder than trying desperately to be the person someone else wants you to be, but failing, and forgetting how to be you in the process.

Divorce is a dirty word I fight hard to keep out of my daily thoughts. Both of our childhoods were riddled with divorce; second, third, even fourth marriages, abusive stepfathers, and too much weirdness. This is the life I have chosen and I desperately want to make it work, make Shane be a good husband, make him stop using drugs, make him healthy, make him treat me right, make him love me the way I need to be loved, not just the hard way he does it.

Shane yells at me more than he talks to me. Sometimes he yells in my face for hours. He gets on a roll and just can't stop. I think it is the drugs talking but his ugly words bruise my mind and leave me breathless and injured. He yells at me if it is raining and he wants sunshine. He yells at me if the brown shirt he wore two hours ago is still dirty because I haven't washed it yet. He yells at me when the traffic light turns red and he has to stop. He yells, shakes his finger in my face and backs me into the corner just to make me cry. Then he yells at me for crying. He'll tell me to get my blubbering face out of his sight and when I try to move toward the door, he yells at me for trying to get away. He yells at me for not sticking up for myself, and then he yells at me for making a pathetic attempt at it.

I am to blame when anything goes wrong. I am not allowed to have an opinion, to fight back, or deny him anything. He is the man of the house, the king of his castle. He reminds me daily that I am his wife, and the Bible says that I must obey him. I don't know enough about what the Bible says or doesn't say to argue with him, but I know in my heart he is wrong. But knowing he is wrong isn't enough. What I need are the words to fight back, the strength, the conviction to speak my mind, but none of that is there for me. I am unable to defend or protect myself. With Shane, I am paralyzed. I stop trying to express how I feel, say what I think; say those things I know to be true but can't find a voice for. I keep those unvoiced fragments of thoughts to myself and get good at not having an opinion. My words get buried so deep inside me that after a while, I forget to think them. I forget that I'm aloud to think, I forget what life is like to use my brain for anything more than worrying about what Shane is thinking or when he's going to yell at me again. I spend all my thoughts and energy on trying to make his world perfect for him.

I make my way through the days of this life I have chosen by getting high. Neither one of us likes the high of meth. I'm sure the reason Shane is able to make so much money from it is because neither one of us uses. My high of choice is marijuana. As long as we have a stash of quality weed, and I can smoke two or three times a day, I am content. Shane, though, will light his next joint with his last one and keep it up all day; on top of the Valium, Quaaludes, Seconal, or whatever other tranquilizer he has on hand. I'll pop a downer now and then too, but generally, I like to be just high enough to be able to ignore my reality.

All around us, people are doing the speed; snorting it, eating it, shooting it. There is a steady flow of them coming to our house and they don't leave for hours. Some stay for days. One night I find this guy in our garage waxing my car at two o'clock in the morning. The same guy is on his hands and knees with a wet rag cleaning the baseboards in my dining room an hour later. Shane and I are renting a three-bedroom, two-bath brick house in a quiet suburban neighborhood and it is a miracle that our neighbors have never called the police. Cars come and go at all hours of the day and night, people are shooting up everywhere, the marijuana smoke is so thick you could cut it with a knife, and our huge stereo speakers strain under the constant blast of Bob Seger, The Rolling Stones, Led Zeppelin, Lynyrd Skynyrd, ZZ Top, or Willie and Waylon twenty-four hours a day. I walk into my own bedroom and find total strangers – junkies – sitting on my bed with needles in their arms. To get any sleep I have to leave and find a motel.

Shane is sitting alone on the floor in the extra bedroom we call the office, turning piles of messy money into tidy white envelopes; obsessively smoothing out all the bills, fixing dog-eared corners, making sure they all face the same direction. His Gold Cup is on the carpet next to his right hip. When I bend down to kiss him goodbye he shoves a wad of cash into my purse. There's still a few hundred in my wallet from the last time I had to leave. All my life I've never had money and now my purse is full of it and I don't know what to do with it. As I stand and turn to go Shane tells me what a fine ass I have and it makes my heart hurt. I don't want to leave, to go out into the dark, drive around and find some place to sleep. I want to make all the junkies go home so we can have our house back to ourselves. But I don't know how to say what I think and how I feel, so I go because I have to get away from the craziness, the incessant noise and the negative energy emitted by a houseful of people strung out on speed. There's a palpable, magnetic, almost electric pull that tries to suck you in, suck you down into the mire of demons smothering their grasp on what's real. Speed junkies live in a frantic, paranoid state of prickliness and if you get too close or stay too long you will get sucked in and you will be destroyed by their black energy. The devil swims through the veins of a junkie. I've seen his evil in their eyes, heard his voice in their words many times and I run.

We rent a safety deposit box and fill it with tidy white envelopes. I keep the key in my wallet. My hands sweat each time I go to the bank, my purse bulging with envelopes to add to our growing fortune of drug money. I have to sign in at the safety deposit desk each time and the pen sometimes slips from my wet fingers. Shane gives lots of the money to friends; we buy new clothes, we eat every day now, and we take trips. One February we spend two weeks in Acapulco. We take huge groups of friends to South Padre Island and Vail, Colorado.

Shane has his pilot's license, and now he has money, so he decides he needs to buy an airplane and one day he comes home with the keys to a Piper Cherokee Six. He flies us places now and it's scary because a big part of me doesn't truly believe he knows what he's doing, although we never crash; unless you count the time we land on a snowy runway in Athens, Texas and skid off the runway, snow packed so tight in the wheel wells that they won't turn any more. We're stuck there for three days waiting for the snow and ice to melt. And then there's the really hot summer day he can't quite get us on the ground. The wheels hit the runway and we bounce back up, then we hit the runway again and bounce back up, over and over again. I am frozen with fear as I watch the end of the runway approaching quickly, a thick row of hedges coming straight at us. It's a miracle we don't plow right through those bushes. Somehow, right when we're out of chances, the wheels stay on the ground and we grind to a halt just a few feet from the shiny green leaves.

But there are a few good times in the sky with Shane at the helm. I will never forget the two summers we take to the skies on July 4th to watch fireworks from above. I am so enthralled with viewing the bursts of color from this new angle that I forget any fear or trepidation I might have about my pilot's abilities. There are several displays going simultaneously and no matter where you look, there are more and more loud booms, sparks of glitter and blasts of red, white, and blue fire shooting up toward us and exploding again and again; magic in the night sky. We scream with excitement, clap our hands, ooooh and awww like children, and then we are moved to silence; reminded of just how lucky we are to live in this beautiful, free land of ours.

We spend like the money is growing on a tree in our yard. I go to the mall and buy anything I want and Shane spends money like crazy on our cars. The Blazer is in the shop every other week getting some new fog light or lift kit or super shocks installed. The Corvette we've had for a few years gets everything fixed and we keep them both shiny and clean. We're living high on the hog but I feel more and more unhappy. There is a black cloud hanging over my head. The money feels dirty and there is little joy in spending it. I wish more and more that we were normal, that I wasn't ashamed of how Shane made the money, that I had some direction and purpose to my life.

I'm yearning for a baby even though the conditions are not right for a child. My naive hope is that a baby will change everything, even Shane. I'm not on birth control any more but can't seem to get pregnant. I go to doctor after doctor and they all tell me I probably won't be able to have children because of my cystic ovaries, and the endometriosis that slams me with stabbing pain out of the blue almost daily. But I pray for a baby anyway. Something inside me desperately needs to give birth to a pure and sweet and perfect child. I promise God I will love my baby like no other mother in the history of the world has ever loved a child. I know I will be a good mother and I pray that Shane will change his ways if we have a baby; surely he won't deal drugs in a house where we're trying to raise our own precious child. Surely.

Chapter Six

A year goes by. A year of life in the fast lane with lots of money and we finally move out of the rent house in town. Shane's paranoia has maxed out. He is now convinced we are being watched and is sure the cops are listening to our calls, so he finds and leases some property out in the country. Ten secluded acres in Wise County. There is an old run-down trailer house, a big barn, a chicken coop, and a huge garden plot. There is no phone line and Shane likes it that way. Shane decides that it is secluded enough that we can live there and he can cook his speed there too every few months when we need to make more money. He and his buddies buy a big, prefabricated barn and put it out there next to the trailer. We store all of our furniture and boxed belongings in the barn for the time being and live in the old, furnished trailer with the ratty gold shag carpet, a gold crushed-velvet sofa and a heavy, Mexican-style wood coffee table in the living room. In the kitchen there is a yellow Formica table and two matching chairs that is the spitting image of the one my parents had when I was growing up. The one that mama would sit at, smoking cigarettes and talking on the phone while she swatted me away like a fly. One bare light bulb hangs over the center of the table. One bedroom is empty and in the other one, we throw a double-size mattress on the floor and use a cardboard box for a nightstand. We stack other cardboard boxes on their sides, so the openings face outward, forming a series of cubby holes, and use them as a dresser for our clothes.

It is great being out in the country, far away from the junkies. Our dog, a black lab named Dino loves running wild. A friend brings his dog out there too, also a black lab, and Dino is in heaven. Those dogs play, run, swim, hunt and have the time of their lives. For several months it is bliss; just me, Shane and the dogs living quietly, taking long walks in the woods and going fishing. Shane and I have never spent so much quality time together. It is nice. We are relaxed out here away from the city. Shane actually talks to me and hardly ever yells. He tells me things I've never known about him and I fall in love all over again. We sit in lawn chairs under the stars and listen to the crickets and the hoot of an owl. We sleep soundly and make love loudly and shower together every day. Shane finds an old tiller in the barn and after a day of tinkering on it, has it running like a top. He tills up the huge half acre garden plot for days and the earth is rich and fragrant; I sit in the big middle of the loose dirt grabbing handfuls and letting it sift through my fingers like all-purpose flour. We plant every kind of vegetable you can think of and revel at each tiny, green shoot that sprouts from the ground. We buy rolls of chicken wire and patch up the pens and fill them with chickens, turkeys and geese. We spend the spring mending fence, planting flowers, and sprucing up the place.

One day I am the only one home and I'm mowing the front lawn barefooted. I decide to go inside and put on some shoes before I try to mow the backyard where the grass is six inches high.

I turn off the mower, run inside, grab a pair of socks out of the sock cubbyhole, and my tennis shoes from the closet and sit on the edge of the bed to put them on. As I'm tying the last lace, a large plastic thermos suddenly tumbles down from a shelf in the closet and lands at my feet. I jump up and look into the closet to see why the thermos would have fallen and I'm eye to eye with a huge chicken snake, as big around as a can of Coke, coiled and stacked on the shelf like a garden hose. I run into the living room, grab the .22 that stands in the corner by the door, and run back into the bedroom. But the snake is gone. I can't find him anywhere. Still holding the small rifle, I poke the tip of the barrel into each cubbyhole over and over, making a mess of the clothes in each box. I shake the bed covers and even turn the mattress upside down searching for him. I search the adjoining bathroom, the shower and the cabinets, all to no avail. After a while, I give up and go back outside to finish the lawn. A few days later, out in the yard, Shane takes his .45 and shoots a chicken snake matching the same description. This one has a duck egg in its mouth and egg splatters everywhere.

Shane rigs up a shop in the old barn and we pull the engine out of the Blazer and take it apart. Shane wants to rebuild it so it will have more horsepower. I marvel at how he knows what each piece is and where it goes and it is great fun being there with him, handing him a 3/16s or whatever other tool he asks for. I've gotten real good at identifying car parts and tools since I've been with Shane and he praises me when I give him the right one. Sometimes we make love on a blanket right there in the barn with the car parts and the tools and the smell of grease and gasoline all around us.

And then it is time to cook the speed and the magic is gone.

I'm not comfortable being there so I take off for a few days each time the chemicals, Bunsen burners, glass tubing and all the other necessary lab paraphernalia shows up. One of Shane's associates keeps it all buried in the ground somewhere that neither one of us knows. I spend lots of time visiting family, driving through the countryside, staying in motels; just being alone. It is a lonely, miserable life and I would trade it in an instant for a quiet, normal life with an empty wallet.

Spring gives way to the heat of the summer and by June our garden is bursting with ripe tomatoes, okra, corn, radishes, onions, carrots, beets, cabbage, three kinds of lettuce, five varieties of peppers, cantaloupe and watermelon. Our large goose squawks and hisses, nipping at my ankles as I walk to the garden to fill up my basket each morning. We eat wonderful, fresh meals for weeks just from our garden, and I can and freeze as much of the produce as I can. One day I fill it quickly and decide the rows need a little working, so I grab the hand-tool hanging on a nail on the side of the chicken coop and start on one of the five rows of tomatoes. I move down the row, lifting up the fragrant branches so I can loosen and work the dirt around the base of each plant. I'm on the last row of tomatoes closest to the fence, moving methodically, enjoying the morning, the exercise and the fresh air. I lift the branches of the next plant and see a pile of straw. Without thinking, I lift the straw and toss it to the side, revealing a bowl-shaped depression in the ground that is full of hairless, newborn rabbits. Their eyes are still closed, but there's no mistaking those ears. Quickly, I replace the pile of straw and let the branches fall gently back into place. When I check on them the next day they are gone, and I'm filled with a sense of doom.

After the baby rabbits disappear, I lose interest in the garden. I can't let myself be responsible for disturbing any more delicate lives, disrupting mother nature's plan, so I don't pick any more tomatoes, I ignore the corn and okra, let the carrots rot in the ground. Soon the weeds take over and I don't even look in that direction. The grass in the yard dries and turns brown, the flowers wilt; the magic of our country oasis is gone like the baby rabbits are gone and nothing but oppressive, heavy heat fills the days and nights. I feel weighed down by the emptiness of my life; I yearn for direction and purpose. Summer has taken the promise of springtime and smothered the life from all that surrounds me. Shane goes off and stays gone for days; I have no idea where he is or what he's doing. When we do see each other, it's a brief, sweaty encounter all prickly and hot and uncomfortable. Shane is yelling at me again; it's my fault it's so damn hot and everything is dying. Neither one of us can breathe so we drive off in separate directions; Shane in the Blazer and me in the Vette, both vehicles black and hot and doomed.

I never go back there to the trailer in the country. I never see the dogs again or have the goose nip at my ankles. I know my marriage is over and I have no desire to see Shane or hear his harsh words. I spend a week driving around and staying in motels dreaming of a new, normal life on my own. For the first time, I seriously consider divorce; it no longer feels like a dirty word. I was built for a respectable, quiet life where I don't have to look over my shoulder. I want it, I need it, I dream of a life I can be proud of. I crave safety, security and peace. I desperately want and need a life that doesn't make me reach for a joint every few hours just to chase away the demons. I have finally had enough. I know I can do this. So, in late June of 1985 I show up on my baby sister's doorstep and move into her one-bedroom apartment with her.

After about a week Shane calls to see where I am. I tell him I'm not coming back to the farm; that I'm going to get a job and be on my own.

He says we'll see.

It has been four years since I've worked. Four years of smoking pot and taking pills. The prospect of re-entering the job market is my first step toward a normal life. I buy the right clothes and go on job interviews. I get a call back for a second interview at a flight-training center at Meacham Field and am overjoyed when they offer me the job. I am to start my new job as an executive secretary the following Monday. It has been a couple of weeks since I've seen or spoken to Shane. Things are looking up and I am feeling stronger than ever.

The next day is Friday. My sister gets up early and goes out to the pool to get some sun before she has to go to work later that morning. I have been up for a while; fresh out of the shower, I'm pouring myself a bowl of cereal when there is a quick, hard series of knocks on the front door. Who knows what course my life may have taken if I had not opened the door for Shane that morning.

Chapter Seven

He is frantic. He comes in and closes the door behind him so quickly he almost knocks me over. His hair has been cut short, his beard is gone and he's wearing cut-off blue jean shorts, a t-shirt I've never seen and tennis shoes with no socks. Before he speaks he moves over and closes the mini blinds on the living room window.

His movements are jerky and sharp and he is buzzing like a live wire. Something terrible has happened and the hint of its ramifications begins seeping into my veins like a toxic chemical before he has even spoken a word. I feel it before knowing it that life has been altered, that something monumental has shifted and that we are at a crossroad so significant nothing will ever be the same. I put up all my defenses and try desperately not to be pulled back on board the roller coaster that is Shane's life.

As if he can sense my defensiveness, he turns from the window and barks that I have to get my stuff. We have to get out of here now and he says it like he's not going to tolerate any shit from me.

I'm afraid of him, but not like I used to be. I've been away from him for several weeks, I'll be starting my new job in a few days, I'm brazen in the comfort of my autonomy and I tell him that I don't want to go anywhere and I ask what's going on.

The cops raided the lab last night. I've been running from them all night. Let's go! He grabs at my arm but I'm just out of reach and am able to pull away.

Oh God. I've known deep down that this was going to happen eventually, and here it is. But I've escaped being involved, I wasn't there, I haven't been out there in weeks. I'm safe. I'm starting a new life. Things are turning around for me. I'm not a part of this terrible thing that has happened. My mind tells me all this in the blink of an eye and I'm desperate to focus on bright thoughts, positive truths, but a dark yarn has already begun threading itself around me and I am choking for air. I manage to verbalize questions that I don't really want answers to.

What are you going to do? Why'd you come here? Why didn't you just leave town?

He stands there for a second looking at me like he doesn't know who I am. I can hear the sounds of summer outside the window, the drone of the air conditioning units, a water sprinkler hitting the window screen with intermittent sweeps, and I can hear him breathing hard.

His face softens. He flashes me a quick smile and moves closer to me. Backing up as much as I can in the tiny apartment I find myself pinned against the bar separating the kitchen from the living room and he is still coming closer. Instinctively, my hands fly up, palms facing out, my upper body leaning back over the bar.

Shane, if they're looking for you, you shouldn't be here. You need to get as far away as you ca...

Shane's mouth covers mine in a hard kiss, his insistent tongue invading my mouth. He grabs me around the waist with both his hands and presses his lean, muscular body against me. My open palms land weakly on his chest. I can feel him grow hard as he rocks his hips against me suggestively and a wave of repulsion swims through every cell of my body.

I've missed you baby, he breathes into my ear. I want to be inside you.

Shane, STOP! I beg, trying to free myself from his grasp. Let me go. I don't want you... and just like that he stops.

He pulls his head back and I see his face fall into a hard frown. And in an instant there is wickedness in his cold eyes. Sparks of green fire jump out at me. His hands slide from my waist down to my ass and possessively, violently, he picks me up and sits me on the bar. I know I am not allowed to fight him anymore.

Chapter Eight

What's going to happen to all our stuff that's stored in the barn?

All of my personal belongings, except what little I have with me, are packed in boxes and stored in a barn at the farm the cops have just raided. Our furniture and our washing machine, all of our dishes, linens, everything is in that barn; and just as quickly as my own question hits my ears, I realize how silly it sounds. I know that I will never see any of my stuff again. This truly is going to be a whole new life for me. I'm starting completely over. Everything is gone. All my photo albums, my high school yearbooks, scrapbooks, keepsakes, jewelry, clothes; all the 'things' of my life are gone.

This reminds me of my childhood. When I was growing up, we moved an average of once every two years, sometimes more often. Each time we moved from one Air Force base to another, a lot of my stuff would disappear. My three sisters would also have less stuff when we arrived at the new house on the new base in the new state. We literally started over with each move. Not only were we the new kids on the block, the new kid in our classrooms; we no longer had our Chatty Kathy's, our Mrs. Beasley's, our box of 64 Crayons and favorite coloring books, our record players or our Donny Osmond posters. In times of stress, we had precious little of what was familiar and comfortable to hold on to.

I feel the familiar heaviness of loss sitting like an elephant on my chest as Shane drives. We're in a friend's truck that Shane has borrowed for this mission of collecting me. Shane is irritated that I'm thinking about the stuff in the barn.

We've got a lot more important shit to think about godammit!

I can tell he is exhausted. He still hasn't told me any more about the raid but I can tell this is not the time to ask questions.

Charlie and a couple other friends are sitting around the living room and are just firing up a joint when Shane and I walk in the front door. It's almost noon. The mood in the small room is somber. There is a half empty bucket of fried chicken on the coffee table; paper plates, napkins and drink cups are scattered on and around the glass-topped coffee table. I nod at Charlie and take a seat at the end of the couch nearest the door. Shane sits on the floor in front of me, wedging his shoulders between my knees and reaches into the bucket for a piece of extra crispy. The TV is on with the volume muted and the stereo is turned way down. It seems as if everyone in the room is as anxious as I am to hear details about the raid and it isn't long before Shane puts down what's left of the piece of chicken, licks his fingers and starts talking.

It's late, probably around 2:00. I'm sitting at the table in the trailer, rolling a couple of joints for the road when the fucking dogs start barking. I reach up and unscrew the light bulb over the table, grab my .45 and go outside to see what the fuck. Carlos, Bobby and Kurt all left before midnight, so I'm the only one there. I see a car coming slow down the driveway, no headlights. At first I think it's just one of the guys coming back for something, but as the car gets closer, I can tell it's not one of them, so I shoot one shot in the air to try to scare away whoever the fuck it is. They must think I'm shooting at them cause all of a sudden, lights are flashing and the motherfuckers are fucking shooting at me. Bullets are flying over my head and digging into the dirt behind me and I'm running like shit toward the creek.

Holy shit! Charlie says, passing Shane a joint, how'd you get away, man? It's been on the news all morning. They've got fucking dogs, helicopters and every motherfucker in the county looking for you.

They don't know it's me they're fucking looking for. Shane is defensive as he takes another hit before passing me the joint. All they have is fucking circumstantial evidence. No one knows it was me there. They can't prove a thing.

They said on the news that they found your wallet in the trailer.

Fuck em. Circumstantial. My name is on the lease, but no one fuckin saw me, it was too dark. They don't have shit.

They've got the dope, man.

They only got some of it, the guys left with over two pounds. It's no big deal. We'll just have to find another place to cook next time. This ain't shit.

Shane is up pacing the floor now, talking shit, trying hard to believe what he's saying. He grabs my knee and gives it a squeeze as if he's marking his last words with an exclamation point. I don't give him the cute giggle he is expecting and I avoid making eye contact with him and reach into the bucket for a wing.

Shane continues with his story, telling us how he ran through the woods behind the trailer, along the creek, up a hill, down into a canyon, over a cliff, across another creek; swimming, lying under the water, dodging man, police dogs and fucking helicopters. Then he explains how, after daybreak, he finds a country road and just starts walking; he can hear a helicopter in the near distance. Pretty soon an old rusty truck pulls up and this guy offers him a ride. Shane says the guy had heard about the manhunt on the radio and was honored to help him get away from the fucking pigs. Once at this guy's house, they get high, Shane takes a shower, shaves his beard, cuts his hair and borrows a shirt. Then Shane calls and asks Charlie to come get him.

Hey, turn up the TV, the news is on.

We watch in silence as the local newscasters bring us the day's headlines in 20-second sound bites. Toward the end of the broadcast there is a ten second blurb about an ongoing manhunt in Wise County but that the Sheriff's department has released few details. No pictures, no names, no big deal. Shane laughs.

It ain't nothin but a thang.

He has outsmarted the law again. It isn't the first time; it probably won't be the last. Another joint is rolled and passed around the room, then Shane announces that he is tired and wants to sleep for a few hours. Charlie says the guest room is ours. Shane grabs my hand, I grab my purse and bag and we head down the hall.

The tiny room is sparse and stuffy. There is a mattress on the floor, an alarm clock and an old lamp on a stack of *Playboy Magazines* beside the bed. There is a yellow plastic 3-tiered shelving unit against one wall that is crammed full of paperback books and more Playboys. On the floor in the corner by the closet is a dusty oscillating fan, pointed toward the foot of the mattress. I turn it on and now it is buzzing softly on its lowest speed. The one small window above the bed is covered with a vinyl pull-down shade. There are sheets and a blanket laying in a tangle on the mattress.

Shane quickly takes off his clothes and falls onto the mattress. I take a seat on the far edge of the bed.

Get over here. Shane grabs me by the waist and pulls me down next to him. We're going to sleep now. He wraps himself around me, pinning me between his body and the mattress. Within a few minutes he is breathing the slow steady breath of sleep. Shane has always liked to hold on tight to me while he sleeps. It's tough sometimes for me to just turn over and try to get comfortable because he's got his arms wrapped around me like I'm some kind of security blanket or something.

Eventually I doze off and must sleep for a few hours because when my eyes fly open the room is dark. Shane has turned on his back, his left arm no longer holding me tightly. His right arm is still under me, but that hand now lies loosely on the bed instead of curled tightly around my middle. After a few minutes my eyes grow accustomed to the darkness. Slowly I pull myself to a sitting position and scoot to the end of the bed, careful not to bump against his legs.

Where are you going? Shane's voice is wide-awake.

I need to use the bathroom. Shane lets me go. I open the bedroom door and walk across the hall into the bathroom. After I flush, I wash my hands and face, find a clean towel in the cabinet and stare at my reflection in the mirror for a long time. I look different; older, sad, hollow. The corners of my mouth droop as if being pulled down by invisible strings, like a puppet. That's how I look. That's how I feel.

The lamp beside the bed is on when I come back into the room. The lampshade is yellow and the room is bathed in the soft yellow glow; everything looks better than it really is. Shane is sitting cross-legged in the middle of the bed. The air is prickly with his edginess.

You think you're really gonna leave me, don't you?

His question stops me cold. All I want is to get out of there. Please God, just get me out of this room and away from Shane. Don't let me get mixed up with him again. Please, dear God.

The silence lasts too long. I don't want them to, but my eyes move from my wringing hands to the tears running down Shane's face. That's not what I expect to see. I am prepared for a cold stare or even a sneer. I am prepared for harsh words, but the tears throw me for a loop. I have only seen Shane cry once in all the years we've been together. It was the night he told me about his childhood; about his mother leaving him at the hospital when he was born, about his grandmother raising him, and about having to run away at 14 years old for shooting his step-dad. After he had told the entire story, there were a few tears when he admitted that he worries about his little brothers and sisters that he had to leave behind in that hellhole. He has never cried for me. I have left this man six or eight times over the years and never has he shed one tear or even acted sad. He has always been confident that I would be back. Something is different now.

I silently attribute these tears to a culmination of the myriad of emotions he must have swallowed over the past 18 hours. He has been through quite an ordeal. Maybe it's just all catching up with him and he's not able to hold it in any more.

Whatever it is I am determined to stay strong in my resolve, to not let him suck me back in. But already, just being in his presence, I am weaker. Sleeping all day, not eating right, the revelation of having most likely just lost all of our belongings are beginning to take their toll. I am hungry, scared and edgy. Now, on top of all that, Shane is crying.

Shane, you know it's time for us to go our separate ways.

My voice is not convincing even to my own ears. I'm staring at my hands afraid to look at him for fear I'll start crying too.

Just then Charlie blasts into the room without knocking telling us we need to come watch the news. They have just shown Shane's picture on the 10:00 o'clock news and are coming back with the story after the commercial break.

The other friends are gone, the bucket of chicken is gone and Charlie has cleared away the mess and emptied the ashtrays. Now Charlie and I are sitting on the edge of the couch leaning toward the television in anticipation and Shane is pacing the floor. We are all waiting in silence, watching the commercials without watching them.

I'll never forget that it is the Channel 5 anchors whose bright faces bring our world to a screeching halt on that hot July night. First, they show Shane's driver's license picture. It looks so huge on the TV screen; ten times bigger than life and it is hard to look at. The male news anchor is describing Shane as the man wanted for attempted capital murder of a Wise County Sheriff's deputy; that there is still an ongoing manhunt with police and sheriff's departments from six neighboring counties participating. I am still reeling from this news and cannot believe when they show my picture next. It is a recent photo they must have taken from a family album I left at the trailer. They give my name and physical description and identify me as the wife of the suspect. I am covering my gaping mouth with both my hands because I cannot believe what I am seeing. I cannot believe what I am hearing. There are taped interviews of so-called witnesses; one of a Wise County deputy who, in a serious Texas drawl explains how he had seen me and Shane in town earlier that evening – together!

I blurt out that he needs is eyes examined. I wasn't there I yell at the TV.

The report goes on for way longer than thirty seconds. This is no sound bite. There is footage of the driveway where the deputies had been 'shot at', the exterior and interior of the trailer, the baggies of the white powdery substance found on the premises, and numerous snapshots of our friends and family taken on happier days; more photos taken from our albums. One such shot had been taken in jest with all of us dressed in camouflage clothes and holding guns. They took what was a spontaneous, fun gathering of friends goofing around and made it look and sound like we were a dangerous group of militant soldiers on the warpath. The story goes on and on and right before my eyes, in living color, I watch my life disintegrate. My mind is reeling. Was I that person they have painted with their well-chosen photographs, fancy words and unreliable witnesses? The web they are weaving with the pieces they have found is skewed and obscenely wrong and I feel suddenly violated and defensive. How dare they tell these lies! People are going to believe what they are seeing and being told on TV. How am I ever going to face the world again?

I don't. Not for a long time.

Chapter Nine

Bob Seger is singing *Against The Wind* as I count white lines in the darkness. The road hypnotizes me and counting keeps my mind off the real stuff vying for my attention.

My hands have begun to itch between my fingers and I am rubbing them together in my lap, which stops the itching for a second, but then it comes back with a vengeance. The chaos of the day has brought back my nervous rash; only this is a grown-up version of the rash I used to get when I was a child.

We left Charlie's house immediately after watching the story that has changed our lives. Once he'd seen enough of the bullshit broadcast Shane jumped off the couch and said fuck this fuckin shit. Motherfuckin assholes don't know their asses from a hole in the ground. Shit! Motherfucker! Charlie, give me a gym bag and some clothes. Vanessa, get your shit. We're getting the hell outta Dodge, baby. Motherfucking cocksuckers. Charlie, I need your truck, man.

And we're gone just like that. There is no discussion about whether or not I will go with Shane. It is understood loud and clear that we are both fugitives according to the law and their so-called witnesses. We both saw it on television, along with the rest of the Dallas/Fort Worth area. Neither one of us is safe here.

Shane has the cruise control set on 55 mph. We fill the gas tank on the way out of town and buy a bag of groceries and drinks for the road. Shane drives cautiously through town; coming to full and complete stops, using his turn signals and not taking any chances.

Twelve hours later, we check into a Motel 6 on the outskirts of Denver and sleep for a day and a half.

After a long, hot shower and a big breakfast, Shane tells me I must drive back to Texas by myself, get all of our money out of the safety deposit box, give Charlie his truck back, and fly back to Denver as fast as I can.

I do exactly as he says and am back at the Motel 6 in less than 24 hours with 23 little white envelopes.

I drive straight through from Denver to Fort Worth (about 12 hours) and go directly to Charlie's house. He takes me to the bank where I efficiently empty the contents of our box into my purse and walk out. I am scared to death and more nervous than ever, but everything goes smoothly. Charlie then drives me to the airport and I fly back to Denver using a fake name that comes to me just as I approach the American Airlines ticket counter to purchase my ticket with cash. No ID check, no security, no questions asked.

The look of shock on Shane's face when he opens the motel room door and sees me standing there tells me that he never expected to see me again. He is in awe. He grabs me, pulls me into the room and holds me tight for several minutes. It means more than everything to him that I have just done what I've done. It is during this desperate hug that it occurs to me for the first time that I could have stayed in Texas, kept the money and started my new life without him. In fact, I think he expected me to do just that. But

I didn't. I was a loyal, honest and obedient wife and I came through for him in his darkest hour. The silent, emotional hug is my only reward.

At some point over the next few miserable hours in the Motel 6, Shane comes to the conclusion that the only place for us to go is Alaska. We will take a bus from Denver to Seattle and fly from there to Anchorage. That is the extent of our plan.

For the next five days, we are on one grimy Greyhound bus after another, stopping in every small town along the way. I age a lifetime on that bus as flashbacks of all the unpleasant things Shane has brought into my life play over in my mind like a bad movie.

There is the Valentine's Day when Shane comes home with two identical bouquets of flowers. He walks in the door all smiling and happy, tells me Happy Valentine's Day as he hands me one of the bouquets. As I read the card he gives me a quick, hard kiss. Then he's out the door with the other bouquet and doesn't come home all night.

Once, he brings his girlfriend home with him and lets her sleep on our couch because she is afraid her husband will beat her if she goes home. He insists that I fix breakfast for the three of us the next morning.

To his credit, Shane never lies to me. If I muster up the courage to ask, he answers honestly. He knows I am right where he wants me, broken, weak and insecure.

One of my worst and most humiliating experiences is the time I get busted and spend a night in jail.

Shane has just bought a pound of pot from some guy. He's going to make a mint selling ounces.

The guy who sells it to Shane gets pulled over by the police shortly after leaving our duplex. The cops find several more pounds in the trunk of his car. A friend drives by, sees the bust and calls to warn Shane. Shane decides to take all the pot, the scales, and all of our paraphernalia, and leave the house just in case this guy narks. I stay home where I'll be safe.

About an hour later I am lying on the couch wearing only a t-shirt and panties, half asleep, watching David Letterman. The room is dark except for the glow of the television.

BANG! BANG! BANG! Someone is pounding on the door.

Police, open up!

Scared to death, I jump up and am standing in the middle of the room not sure what to do. There is a small, uncovered window in the front door and I can see an angry face staring in at me.

Police! Open the door! We have a search warrant.

Instead of opening the door I run down the hall toward the bedroom to grab a pair of jeans first. They don't wait. Seconds later I hear the front door, then the back door being kicked in and immediately the two-bedroom, 750 square-foot duplex is swarming with angry armed police officers; some in uniform, some not; guns pointing at me from every direction and everyone is yelling at me.

Put your hands on your head! An undercover officer screams, his gun two feet from my face.

I do as he says. He holsters his gun and grabs my right hand and spins me around, twisting my arm behind me and I am cuffed. With one hand, he is pulling my cuffed hands up between my shoulder blades and my shoulders feel like they will tear out of their sockets; his other hand feels for whatever he thinks I could be hiding under my t-shirt. My face and chest are smashed against the cool, painted drywall and he uses one of his feet to spread my legs far apart and away from the wall.

What's your name? Do you live here? Who else lives here? Where's Shane? Where's the dope? It'll be easier on you if you tell us what we want to know.

Someone has found my purse and driver's license so now they know my name, but I refuse to answer any of their questions. And while this guy continues to bark questions at me, to threaten and insult me; the army of others proceed to tear the house upside down. The couch and chair cushions are torn apart and thrown aside. Tables and chairs are toppled, the underside of every surface is scoured. Every drawer and cabinet in the kitchen is rifled through and emptied onto the floor. The contents of the garbage are inspected. The bathroom and bedrooms are equally assaulted. The army gets madder by the minute when they don't find what they're looking for.

I remain silent and am led to the kitchen and pushed into a chair. A woman cop sits in the chair beside me, and starts talking like we're old friends. Now I am just angry. I'm angry, they're angry, and Shane drives by out front and he is angry too.

An hour later they read me my rights, let me put on a pair of jeans and take me to the station because their search isn't totally unproductive. While searching the garbage they find what they believe to be a couple of marijuana stems and seeds and from the bedroom they find $900 cash hidden between the frame and the mattress of the waterbed. From a dresser drawer, they produce a baggie containing a handful of assorted pills.

The next day around noon one of Shane's buddies springs me. No charges are pressed, they keep the money and the pills, and I get to go home to a monumental mess. It is great to be free, but freedom doesn't erase from my memory the horror of watching my home being torn apart, of being handcuffed and dragged away at gun point, of being fingerprinted and having a mug shot taken. Freedom doesn't lessen the humiliation of having spent a miserable sleepless night in a freezing cold holding cell with several scary women and one filthy stainless steel toilet in the corner.

There's something about riding on a bus that makes you dirty. Maybe it's the diesel fumes. Maybe it's being in such close proximity to too many people. Maybe it's a combination. Whatever it is makes me crazy. We don't stop anywhere long enough to take a shower on our way to Seattle, so I get real creative in the rest rooms of the gas stations along the way. At the same drug store where I stock up on anti-itch creams and sprays for my rash, I buy shampoo, a huge container of Johnson's Baby Powder, cotton balls and astringent, moisturizing cream, mouthwash, and deodorant. At least twice a day, when the bus pulls into another small town for any length of time, I drag my bag to the nearest ladies room and, using brown paper towels from the dispenser, give myself a makeshift sponge bath, wash my face (and my hair if there is time), reapply the deodorant, powder and moisturizer, brush my teeth, rinse with mouthwash and begrudgingly climb back into my seat so the Greyhound can make me dirty all over again.

Before long the rhythm of the road lulls me back to remembering. Remembering some of the roads I've traveled over the years that led me to this one - this road that is taking me farther and farther from my home, my family and my friends.

Chapter Ten

One road I re-travel in my mind is the road that takes me to Spencer's Corner, a popular dance club in Fort Worth, one muggy summer Saturday night in 1978. The night I meet Shane.

It has been a big month for me. I have just turned 18, graduated from high school, am registered to start business school in August, and my father has just told me (in his own quiet way) that it is time for me to move out on my own.

Daddy and Donna, my stepmother, are having a house built in north Fort Worth. While it is being built we are living in an apartment in the Mid-Cities. The house is almost finished and I haven't seen it yet. One Saturday morning I am home and daddy asks if I want to go take a look, just the two of us. As we walk from one unfinished room to the next daddy says here is where I'm going to put my recliner and here's the master bedroom, and look at the size of this bathroom, or this is going to be Mary's room, and this is going to be Jeanie's room, and this is going to be my office. It isn't until we are driving back to the apartment that it hits me. In his own way, he has just told me that there isn't going to be a Vanessa's room in the new house. Neither one of us ever puts it into words but I understand the message: it is time for me to find my own place to live because I am a grown up now. This is how it has always been with daddy. He gives you cryptic hints and you figure out what he's trying to say. He isn't much for words.

One night, soon after the unspoken agreement between daddy and me, I am invited to go dancing with the daughter of one of daddy's old Air Force buddies. I don't know how it happens because I don't even know her well. All I can remember is that I put on my Calvin Klein jeans and a halter-top and she drives us to Spencer's Corner on University Drive, a rock and roll bar not to be confused with a disco club called Spencer's Palace a little farther down the road. We arrive around 9:30 pm, make our way through the rowdy crowd to the bar and buy ourselves beers. The music is blasting, people are everywhere, it's dark and smoky and lots of people are already on the dance floor. As I take my first sip from the long neck I take a quick look around the room and find a pair of smoldering eyes looking right at me from across the dance floor. There is something different about this man. Our eyes lock and he nods deliberately at me, smiling with confidence. I am instantly hypnotized. Then, just like in a movie, never taking his eyes off me, he gets up, walks straight over to me, takes my hand, and we are dancing.

The flashing lights, the noisy crowd, the resonance of the music all work in unison to transport the two of us to another world. Our bodies, our rhythms, our tempos synchronize from the first moment. We dance fast. We dance slow. We are instantly and totally lost in the depths of each other. I have never met anyone so full of electricity, so completely appealing in every way. There is a fierce magnetic energy about him. He is so handsome, so strong, so intense; so virile. He commands the attention of everyone in the room, and the envy of all but the most confident of men. His full, light brown hair is streaked with natural blonde highlights, and falls in a wave just to his shoulders. He has a thick, well-trimmed mustache and just the right amount of chest hair presents itself from beneath his tight silky shirt open to the third button. New blue jeans, a brown leather belt and rugged brown leather boots complete the look that is working so well for him. He carries his toned, muscular body like a proud peacock, his chest out, his shoulders square. And, oh how he can dance! He dances with instinctive rhythm, raw sex appeal and the same self-assurance he exudes off the dance floor. We dance exclusively all night, never sitting down and only occasionally taking long, much-needed draws off our respective beers. Conversation is impossible over the constant noise but talking is not important. We do however manage to exchange phone numbers at some point. So totally and completely lost am I in the thrill and excitement of this handsome, charismatic, sexy, smiling man, that I don't even see or talk to the girl who brought me here until she approaches us around midnight and announces angrily to Shane, as she grabs my arm; she's leaving now. I am literally dragged from the smoky, deafening club, into the heat of the summer night; my heart beating to the rhythm of an exciting new drummer.

Chapter Eleven

I cannot get him out of my mind, out from under my skin.

By Sunday afternoon, when he hasn't called, I can't take it anymore. As if in a trance, I open the Spencer's Corner matchbook, study the number and pick up the telephone. A woman answers and I resist the strong urge to hang up.

May I speak to Shane?

Who's this?

This is Vanessa.

Surprisingly, she chirps, Oh hi! Yeah, just a minute.

A moment later he is on the other end of the turquoise Trimline I hold close to my ear.

Vanessa! Hey Baby! I'm so glad you called.

Really? I wasn't sure...

Oh hell yes! I told Lisa you were the only one I wanted to talk to. Hey sexy, I'm coming to get you. Tell me where you live.

I tell him how to find our apartment, learn that he is staying with some good friends, Lisa and Carlos until he gets back on his feet, and that he'll be picking me up in a few minutes on another friend's Harley.

It is all too exciting! He had told Lisa he only wanted to talk to me. Just me! How had I been lucky enough to go dancing at Spencer's Corner the previous Friday night? I'd never even been there before. This must be fate. My time has come. It is my destiny, my great fortune to have met this man.

There is no mistaking that Shane has arrived when my dad, my sisters and I all hear the distinctive thunderous growl of the Harley Davidson pull up out front. Dark sunglasses, wind-blown hair, tight jeans, T-shirt, leather boots, no helmet; my sister's and I watch him park the monstrous bike from the second floor balcony that overlooks the parking lot of the apartment complex. The introductions are brief and awkward. Daddy asks where we are going. Shane says to a party. I grab my purse and we are gone; my arms tight around Shane's slim waist, my blond hair and my restless spirit flying free on the wind of the hot summer night.

Shane is a complex man. He shows me so many different parts of himself that I am in awe. Just beneath the surface of each new side of him swims an ethereal quality familiar to some tender part of me - the broken little girl who sometimes landed on the wrong end of drunken violence. That girl recognizes and is drawn to the dark dangerous edge of Shane in hopes of catching that rare ray of sunshine, the tender moments that will surely come out-of-the-blue often enough to sustain her.

I learn that he is six years older than me, that he's been living in Colorado for several months because he has been in jail, and that it wasn't the first time he'd done time. He tells me that he was a former Chippendale's dancer, that he used to sing in a rock and roll band and has done every kind of job you can imagine from carpentry to truck driving. There are lots of red flags that are easy for me to ignore because I am already convinced he is my destiny. He is so worldly and handsome, he is my exact opposite and I am attracted to him like a magnet. He draws me in and seduces me with the ribbons of his tales and the magic of his touch. It feels like love to me.

Shane is always the loudest, most commanding presence in any room; people are drawn to him, and he is never at a loss for words. He is naturally intelligent and holds a deep, passionate disdain for the law. And he could care less what anyone thinks of him. I meld myself into the girl he thinks I am. Bending and contorting myself into the person someone needs me to be is all I know of love.

I smoked a joint or two in high school before I met Shane; but now drugs are everywhere and anytime we are together I am getting high, floating through time red-eyed and mellow on a blanket of sweet smoke. It will be a few months before I partake in anything stronger - before I swallow pills to make me happy, pills to bring me down, snort cocaine, smoke hashish, and eat sugar cubes laced with a liquid form of psilocybin that take me on a mind-expanding trip to another level of consciousness where colors dance and fear has a face.

Shane and I never have a conventional dinner and a movie date and we are rarely alone but that doesn't matter. We are instantly a couple and right from the beginning I can't imagine being without him. One month after that first Harley ride, in answer to daddy's subtle petition that it is time for me to move out, I pack my things and move in with Shane. He's renting a brand new two-bedroom, one bath duplex with his buddy (the Harley owner) in Arlington, Texas.

There are two identical white brick duplexes side-by-side with a huge concrete slab for one collective front yard/driveway. One huge pecan tree stands tall from its small patch of earth that has escaped being covered in concrete. Ours is the duplex on the far right. A steady flow of young tenants find and make their homes within the walls of these four units. A young married couple with a baby. Single men. College students. We are neighbors, we become friends, we share our dreams, we understand each other's struggles, and we share our drugs. We knock on each other's doors, but let ourselves in. We share meals, rides and trips to the Laundromat. Our apartment becomes the gathering place. Every evening and all weekend long, ours is a revolving door.

School has started and I am working part time at Taco Bell. Shane has been working as a machinist at an aircraft parts manufacturing plant in Grand Prairie making $8.00 an hour. I think I am all grown up. Life is good. We are in love, we have our own place, I am going to business school, we both have jobs, we both have cars (they are barely running) but we are happy, we are making it on our own. We have each other and I think that's all that matters. I begin dreaming of getting married and having babies because that's the way the fairy tale goes. At my first mention of it though, Shane makes it clear he is not ready. And that's okay. I can wait a little while, but I want babies. I want to love them too much and give them things I never had. Our babies will be beautiful, brilliant and bold.

It doesn't take long for me to lose touch with most of my high school friends and with my family who by now, are living in their new home almost an hour away. My two younger sisters are still in high school, flirting with boys and taking pop quizzes. My older sister is working as a bartender and living in Austin with her boyfriend. Weeks go by with no word from my dad, my sisters or my mom, who is living in Florida with her new husband.

Day after day, week after week, I concentrate on my schoolwork and put in my hours at Taco Bell. Sometimes late at night I drift off to sleep thinking about my best friend Connie who is living in a dorm at Stephen F. Austin State University deep in the piney woods of East Texas.

Connie and I meet our sophomore year in high school and are finishing each other's sentences from day one. We share an equal enthusiasm for clothes, Bruce Springsteen, poetry and boys. We make up a game where we open a dictionary, point to a word and we both write a poem about that word. Then we spend the next thirty minutes laughing and marveling at how similar our poems are. Strong, blond and so sure we have it all figured out, the two of us are inseparable sisters of the soul. Both of us are Air Force brats and have grown accustomed to being routinely uprooted and forced to reinvent ourselves at new schools; new best friends to unearth from the sea of unfamiliar faces. We know how lucky we are to have found each other.

Determined not to lose touch, we faithfully write letters back and forth, cryptic snapshots of our new lives. She tells me about impossible classes, difficult roommates, too much work and not enough money. I tell her about going to school, too much work and not enough money but I don't tell her the bad things.

Money is tight but we manage to make ends meet until our cars begin breaking down sometime in those first few months. We go through a comical series of old broken down automobiles in the fall of 1978 after my first car, a 1973 Vega, finally gasps its last breath. Daddy took me car shopping, but I paid the $900 from my own savings. Shane raffles the Vega off in a football pot on a Sunday Cowboy's game and for a $2.00 square, the lucky winner comes and removes it from our front yard; a thick trail of white smoke hanging in the air as evidence of its existence long after it is gone. We make a little money from selling the squares and Shane buys some pot with it. He doubles our money and buys some more. Soon we have a few hundred dollars and we buy another car.

One of the cars we go through that fall is a huge burgundy 1966 Oldsmobile Cutlass Supreme with black leather interior, a real nice car in its day. Late one night while driving home from work (still wearing my smelly brown and gold polyester Taco Bell uniform) the Cutlass just stops. With no power, no steering, no brakes, I coast to a stop on the side of the highway with thick, white smoke billowing from under the hood. Not sure what has just happened and fearful that the whole car might explode, I grab my purse, jump out, and run. After 50 yards or so, I turn around to look at the car and can't even see it through all the smoke. I'm on the turnpike that runs east and west between Dallas and Fort

Worth and the exits are few and far between. I'm not sure exactly where I am, because I've been driving on autopilot and can't remember which exit was the last one I passed. It is after midnight and there is very little traffic. It's also a very dark night and I can't see anything ahead of or behind me on the road. Scared, tired and disoriented, I look around in every direction for some sign of life. Off in the distance, across a field, I can just make out the image of a 7-Eleven store sign. I can't tell how far away it is, but it's the only thing I see so I leave the road and start walking through the grass. It is even darker now. A moonless dark, thick and heavy like velvet drapes. Blindly I put one foot in front of the other, my arms reaching out, going before me but finding only the heavy curtain of the night. I hear but cannot see cows mumbling to each other in the near distance. With the booming sound of my own heartbeat pounding in my ears, I inch myself closer and closer to the familiar red, orange and green sign.

Shane and I don't have a phone at our place but I know he is playing poker at Lisa's house with her boyfriend Carlos and some other guys, so my plan is to call over there. I sit down on the curb outside the store, after the 20 minute walk through the dark, to collect myself and examine the contents of my wallet and purse. No money, no change. I have been afraid of this all along because it isn't unusual for me to be totally broke, but I had hoped that there would at least be some spare change floating around in the bottom of my purse. After resting there for a few minutes I say a silent prayer, square my shoulders and walk into the store to ask the woman behind the counter if I can use the phone.

No. This here phone is only for business. I can't let nobody use it.

My shoulders slump and tears threaten to fill the corners of my eyes but something in me believes that there is good in every one and that if I just explain my circumstances to her, surely she will let me use the stupid phone. I start telling her what has happened to me tonight, the tone of my voice growing thinner and higher as the story progresses. I can see that nothing I'm saying is getting through to her because none of the deep creases in her leathery face have moved and her eyes are alternating their focus between the refried beans smeared on the front of my uniform and the beanbag ash tray, holding her burning cigarette, on the counter.

My words slow, stop, and float away like lost Scrabble tiles. She takes a long draw off the last half inch of her Camel, mashes the cigarette into the ashtray and busies herself with a crossword puzzle; smoke rising from both nostrils like angry serpents. The phone sits within reach on the counter, mocking my desperation but I cannot bring myself to reach over and pick up the receiver. I leave the store in tears.

Alone, exhausted and feeling like a speck of dust in the universe, I sit on the curb and stare into the darkness that has brought me here.

A couple of minutes later, two teen-age boys come out of the store. The blond one looks my direction on the way to their car, but our eyes don't meet. I don't have it in me to ask them for a quarter. They get into their car as I cling tightly to my useless purse and study the dirty asphalt at my feet.   I expect to hear their engine start and see them drive away. But they don't.   After a minute or two one of them gets back out of the car. My tear-streaked face looks up to see that the one with straight blond hair that reminds me of Tom Petty is walking toward me with his hand outstretched.

Here, he says shyly, dumping a handful of coins (mostly sticky pennies) into my hand. It's all we have but it's enough for a phone call.

His last word trails off to the place where uncomfortable lives. He stuffs his now empty hands into his pockets and swishes his head quickly to one side, moving his long bangs out of his eyes. It is a move he probably makes a thousand times a day and I think it is cute. As I stand, he sheepishly kicks the right toe of his black Converse All Stars into the concrete while looking down.

His youthful shyness matches mine and together our shy energies bounce off each other in the warm night air between us like weightless beach balls. I manage a timid thank you; a part of me wanting to give him a hug but my feet won't move and I just don't know how to cross over into his space and make it happen.

Sure, no problem.

Standing slightly straighter, he backs away and heads toward his car where his pinball buddy waits.

Good luck.

One more swish to move his hair out of his eyes again and he climbs into the driver's seat and cranks the engine to life. A bashful smile lightens my face and I find enough bravery to make eye contact and wave good-bye, hoping on some level they understand the depth of my gratitude.

Back inside the store, I triumphantly drop the filthy coins on the counter and count out twenty-seven cents. Without a word, smoking lady pushes the button on the cash register and pulls out a shiny quarter. I leave her there picking up the sticky pennies with her fat, nicotine-stained fingers and go back outside to use the payphone.

An hour later Shane and Carlos come and get me and we tow the Cutlass back to our duplex with a six foot length of nylon strap Carlos keeps in the back of his truck.

Shane is a very good shade-tree mechanic and begins taking the engine apart the next day; me handing him tools and getting him beer, but soon he is cussing about holes in pistons and melted rings. We cannot afford to pay for the many parts it will take to fix the engine so now we are down to one car that barely runs and I need it to go to school. Shane starts carpooling to work with a guy in our complex who has just gotten on at the plant. But it quickly becomes too difficult to juggle things with just one car, so we decide that I should quit my job which is way on the north side of Fort Worth and too far to drive for $5.00 an hour anyway.

Chapter Twelve

It is a long, hungry winter. Shane is not happy with his job. They are trying to push him into a union steward position and he finds himself mired in politics, caught in the thankless void between his buddies and management. I am trying to keep up with my studies and finish my course at the business school so I can get a good office job. We have no money left over from Shane's paycheck after paying rent and utilities, and are lucky to eat once a day. It is during these months when Shane begins his long screaming tirades against me. His words hit me like a leaf blower sending my own words, thoughts and ideas flying in every which direction leaving me wordless and windblown.

One day he's fed up with working and just ups and quits his job. There will be no more paydays. He uses his last paycheck (our rent money) to buy a thousand hits of black mollies. And when they are gone, he pays the rent and buys a pound of pot with what is left and doubles the money again.

That fucking job was a fucking dead end road, baby.

He sits for hours straightening the corners of the dirty money, flattening out the wrinkles and turning them all to face the same direction.

Strutting around the house like a proud peacock, money in hand, he brags about how good he is.

It takes connections, Baby, to do what I do. Not just any motherfucker can make money like this.

It feels silly and useless to complain about where the money comes from so I don't, but the fear is there. It lives deep in those secret folds of my mind along with the other monsters I learned to bury there as a child; making sure, as always, not to let any of it affect the smile on my face.

I spend countless hours alone in our bedroom practicing my shorthand and trying hard to ignore whatever is happening in the living room.

In February I graduate from business school and quickly find an office job at Northern Propane Gas Company where I can use my newly acquired typing, shorthand, 10-key and accounting skills. Refreshed by the pleasure of working again, of earning money, and having a daily routine, the spring and summer of 1979 fly by. The company buys a computer and sends me to Omaha, Nebraska for a week to learn how to use it. It is a huge box that takes up my whole desk and makes me feel important, doing twice the work in half the time. I feel so useful and productive during the day that it is almost enough to help me ignore my home life. More and more often Shane disappears for days at a time, returning with wads of cash or huge quantities of another drug to sell. I have learned to keep my comments to myself and not to ask questions.

The less you know the better off you'll be sweetheart. This is serious fucking shit. Don't fuck with me.

And there are still tender moments between us; those out-of-the-blue times that keep me going. The time I tell him I need to go to the doctor and renew my birth control pills and he tells me to just quit taking them; that our babies will be the smartest, most beautiful babies in the world. The times he reaches over and touches my face ever so lightly with the back of his fingers while we are watching TV, or the lazy Saturday mornings we make love slowly, our eyes locked, while he tells me all the things he loves about me. These are the moments and this is the Shane I try to remember when things get crazy.

By the end of the summer Shane has dealt enough drugs and made enough money to buy himself a new Harley Davidson, and one day he comes home with a one-year old Corvette for me. It isn't something I've asked for or ever dreamed I'd have. The car is beautiful and costs a whopping $8,000. He put $3,000 down and has somehow gotten a loan for the remaining balance. The payment is $220 a month, and is the only bill I have to pay from my paycheck. No matter how good it feels to have a nice car to drive and money for food, I am more and more afraid of the road on which my life seems to be speeding out of control.

Too many months go by with too many drugs, too many strangers and too few out-of-the-blue moments. Shane is gone most of the time and only yells at me when he is home. There is no warm connection between us. I don't know if I love Shane anymore. I can't make sense of the world around me. It is too hard and depressing and so I tell Shane I'm going away for a few days to visit family.

I fly to Florida to visit my mom and her new husband, who is weird and devil-mean. Bald and bearded, long vertical lines crease his greasy face; cold black eyes say no when his lips say yes. His mood changes like the wind and you cannot predict the direction it will blow.

I suspect that he hurts her at night behind their locked bedroom door. Her sad eyes and bruises say it louder than her silence. In the light of day they both pretend like nothing is wrong and I know all too well how to play that game. We talk about the weather in the morning as he scrambles eggs, big chunky gold and diamond rings on each fat pinky. Already I miss my life with Shane.

I spend a lot of time looking at stacks of photographs I've brought to Florida with me. Snapshots of me and Shane together when we first met, photos of our first Christmas when Shane goes to the pawn shop and buys me a tripod for the 35mm camera daddy gave me for graduation, and I buy Shane a brown bath robe from Sears. Shane wears that robe for days after Christmas, naked as a jaybird underneath, people coming and going. I have to beg him to take a shower and let me wash it. It scares me to see him let himself go like this. He has always been so meticulous about his appearance, almost compulsive about cleanliness. Later I realize this behavior is a red flag I just don't understand how to interpret yet.

There are pictures of us with our duplex friends sitting around in our living room getting high and pictures of us cooking out on the grill. There are shots of the Corvette and the Sportster and some of the other vehicles we have gone through. As I flip through that pile of loose photos, putting them in chronological order, the history of Shane and Vanessa unfolds. Our love story; the beginning, the middle... Tears come to my eyes. I don't want this to be the end. We love each other, we look good together; we have had lots of good times.

As a gift for Shane I create a scrapbook album with these photographs, chronicling our year and a half together. Flipping through the pages of the finished album, I know this love story isn't over. The potent magic of the fairy tale erases all the bad stuff from my memory. I miss him and desperately want to go home and make it work, to have his beautiful babies. He is my destiny. How could I have forgotten? My place is with him, nothing else matters.

I mail the scrapbook to Shane with a Christmas card; we share a heartfelt conversation over the phone, and I am back in Texas before the ball drops on Dick Clark's New Year's Rockin' Eve.

Vanessa Foster, 1980

Chapter Thirteen

Because I picked up and went to Florida without warning, I have lost my job and Shane tells me not to worry about getting a new one, so now I have a lot of free time on my hands.

Before I know it, we are getting married. I don't remember him asking, or me saying yes, but it is definitely happening because we've already sent out the invitations.

> *"We invite you to be with us*
> *as we begin our new life together*
> *on Saturday, April fifth*
> *Nineteen hundred and eighty*
> *at seven o'clock in the evening. . ."*

Our wedding is a small fiasco of friends and family at my father's new house. I wear a $25.00 floor length white cotton prairie dress with baby blue flowers on it and a floppy white hat. Shane wears a rented white tuxedo and dark sunglasses. Carlos is the best man in a baby blue tuxedo and dark sunglasses. Connie comes in from the piney woods to be my maid of honor. Her dress and floppy hat are baby blue and almost match the best man perfectly. She comes over early that afternoon and helps me get ready in my little sister, Jeanie's sunny yellow bedroom that I silently envy.

I'm very nervous and worried that I'm making a big mistake, but I don't know how to put my thoughts into words so I don't say anything to anyone, I just keep busy and keep smiling. I have not yet learned how to unscramble the mess in my mind, manage my own thoughts, or acknowledge my emotions and attach them to the events of my life, so I convince myself that I have to marry Shane. Besides, everyone has gone to so much trouble. There are flowers, a cake, napkins with our names printed in silver ink. The permanence of our names printed in ink helps convince me that it's meant to be.

Shane and Carlos both show up late in Quaalude-induced stupors. These pills are so strong we nickname them the elephant tranquilizers. I beg Shane not to take any on the day of the ceremony but as soon as I see him I know he has taken more than one. As my father and I turn the corner from the kitchen into the dining room where everyone waits, I see him there. His feet are wide apart, his left foot slightly forward for balance. He's wearing dark glasses and a wide grin. Carlos isn't much better off but collectively we manage to prop Shane between the two of us. We have to shush him several times during the ceremony. He slurs the vows, says I am instead of I do, and he bursts out in inappropriate, spontaneous laughter more than once. Despite all this, the minister finally pronounces us man and wife and gives Shane permission to kiss his bride.

It is the longest, wettest, sloppiest kiss in the history of time. Shane is all over me. Carlos loses his grip, I am struggling to push Shane off of me, we teeter and wobble like a couple of Weebles, and then we fall down. We fall down. Onto the floor. At our wedding. During the kiss. I am mortified and everyone is in shock. There is a collective Ooohhhh from the small crowd, and then there is earth-shattering silence. You could have heard a baby blink. There is no protocol for this situation, no one knows what to do or say. Time stands still. And then some gracious soul turns on the stereo which instantly puts an end to the awkward moment. People begin talking loudly, clapping, laughing, helping us up off the floor. My cheeks are blazing red as I wipe my face dry with the lace sleeve of my dress. Someone hands me a glass of champagne and an elephant tranquilizer and the rest of the evening is a blur.

There is no honeymoon. We go back to our duplex and sleep off the Quaaludes.

A month later Shane brings a woman home with him in the middle of the night. I find her sleeping on the couch when I get up the next day. I have seen her around. She is a shy, petite blond like me.

And then Shane is there, all smiles, giving us both hugs. The three of us eat the sausage, eggs and biscuits I throw together for breakfast. We sit in silence as the morning sunshine dances in through the open vertical blinds, slicing our weird world into layers of shadow and light.

It isn't long before the cops bust down the door, I spend the night in jail and Shane decides it is time to get out of town, so we move to California. He promises that when we get there he will apply for a real job, lay low for a while, and everything will be fine. He promises.

We don't even clean up the mess the cops made of our duplex. We just take what we can salvage and head west. I drive the Vette and Shane drives a small U-Haul. He leaves his Harley in a friend's garage. Shane talks about trying to get on at one of the large military aircraft manufacturers north of LA and so we drive straight to Palmdale, California and rent the first nice apartment we come to.

We share two glorious weeks of rediscovery; the honeymoon we never had. We walk and talk and dream together. We have picnics in bed and stay up late getting stoned and watching old movies. We hold hands and touch and kiss and laugh, just like in the beginning. Shane is attentive, loving and sweet. We go shopping for brand new furniture and turn our new apartment into a home; discovering each other's decorating preferences. This is the first furniture I have ever picked out and bought new. It is very exciting for me because everything we've ever had has been someone's cast-offs and hand-me-downs. We make friends with some of our new neighbors, share meals and play cards. Finally! The life I've always imagined we could live. No strangers knocking on the door at all hours of the day and night. No house full of drugs. No paranoia.

No one is hiring. I suspect now that Shane might never have intended to get a real job, and probably never actually went and put in his application, but one day he comes home and announces that he is going back to Texas and he'll be back as soon as he has made some money. This goes on for months. He's gone to Texas for weeks, comes home for a week or so, gives me money for rent and plenty more, then is gone again. He is gone more than he is home. Our neighbors feel so sorry for me that they practically adopt me into their family. There is always a place for me at their table and I don't know what I would do without them.

Once after a particularly long absence, Shane flies into LAX, hires a taxi to drive him all the way to Palmdale, doesn't call to let me know he is coming, and surprises me in the middle of the night. He walks into our dark bedroom and switches on the overhead light, startling me awake. I scream. He yells at me to shut up. I think he is disappointed he didn't catch me sleeping with someone else. I've never cheated and he knows it and I think it makes him feel guilty.

He is not in a good mood. I jump up to give him a hug but he pushes me away. He won't even kiss me. He is angry and short-tempered but won't say what he is mad about. He isn't ready to come to bed so I get up and fix him something to eat. We get high and watch some TV. And finally, after several hours, we go to bed.

Once we are settled into bed I begin kissing his neck and shoulder but he irritably pushes me away again saying he isn't in the mood. He is always in the mood so I ask him what's wrong. He starts to get out of bed but I pull him back and beg him to talk to me. By now I am crying and asking what I have done wrong. And then Shane is talking.

I fucked up and got VD.

Oh.

As soon as I finish the Penicillin the doctor gave me, it'll be fine. You'll never know.

But I do know. I knew it before he said anything. I knew it before we got married. This is how it would always be with Shane: his world, his rules; my heart getting broken over and over again.

He is only in town two nights this time and when he leaves again it is a long time before I miss him.

My neighbor helps me find a part-time job working as a secretary. I excitedly tell Shane about the job over the phone and it makes him mad. He says he doesn't need me to work. I say I want to work, need to do something productive, feel like a citizen. He never understands; can't see why I'm not happy sitting around waiting for him to come back.

One day, several months after moving to California, Shane calls from Texas and tells me it's time to move back home. He has already rented us a house in Cleburne and is waiting for me there.

Just call a moving van and have them bring everything here he tells me. You'll love this old farmhouse. It'll be great, baby. I'll see you in a few days.

I call my boss to let him know I won't be coming back, then grab the yellow pages and decide on North American Van Lines because their large red white and blue ad catches my eye first. Two days later they come and pack everything into compact, easy- to-carry boxes, and load everything into a huge moving van. I fill out the papers telling them where to take our stuff and give them cash. They drive off, leaving me in the empty apartment with my one small suitcase and a map of the United States of

America. I stand at the bar and mark the route I'll take with a red magic marker, then go next door to tell my neighbors good-bye. We all cry and hug promising to keep in touch. They try to talk me into staying but I go because Shane told me to.

Setting the Vette's cruise control to 55 mph, it takes me three days to get from Palmdale, California to Cleburne, Texas where I quickly get a job at City Hall working as a secretary to the City Manager, City Attorney and City Secretary.

I drive with a .357 magnum in the passenger seat just in case anyone tries to mess with me. Shane insists. But I get messed with anyway. Some truckers start playing cat and mouse with me on some lonely stretch of highway. First, one truck tailgates me for a while and then passes me. He slows down and I pass him. We do this several times and just when I think I'll floor it and leave him in the dust, there are two more trucks and they won't let me go anywhere. There's one in front of me, one behind me and one in the left lane right beside me and I'm boxed in. I'm really freaking out and there's nothing I can do. They're probably all talking to each other on their CB radios and who knows what they're trying to pull. Suddenly I realize we're slowing down and they force me to exit and pull into a truck stop. My heart is beating out of my chest and I need to think fast. I grab the gun and put it in my purse as they "escort" me to a parking place. I really need to pee and am hungry anyway so I decide what the hell and jump out and run inside where there are at least some other people. The place is packed but I find an empty booth and slide in, wide-eyed and practically hyperventilating. The next thing I know two of the truckers are there asking if they can join me and I don't feel like I have any choice because they sit down without waiting for an answer. I hug my purse in my lap and try to act cool. They buy me a cheeseburger and we talk for a little while. They end up being nice enough guys...probably about ten years my senior and didn't mean any harm. They just saw a good-looking young blond in a black Corvette and decided to have a little fun. I'm able to leave without any problem because they have to get some sleep and can't drive any more until tomorrow.

Vanessa, circa 1981

Chapter Fourteen

Stubby, the Hereford calf was orphaned at birth a few weeks before Shane and I arrive at the ranch in Homer. He is a tough, stubborn little animal with strong survival instincts and he meanders about the grounds the way a curious puppy would. I see him early the first morning on our way from the fifth wheel trailer up to the log cabin to cook my first breakfast; to scramble a dozen eggs, fry a pound of bacon and slice a loaf of homemade bread that starts everyone's day off right. Stubby turns from his mischievous activity beside the greenhouse and snorts his greeting as Shane and I walk by, still wearing the only clothes we own. Wayne said that he and Jillian would go through their closets and find a few things for us to wear since we're about the same sizes. I'm ready for hand-me-downs whether they fit or not because I've been wearing the same clothes now for four days and I desperately need a shower.

It is a tough, slow walk up the hill (about 100 yards) because both my hips are aching. Shane is also stiff from the cold and we have already decided that we will have to get enough firewood down to the wood-burning stove in the mudroom so we can keep a fire stoked and burning through the night if we're going to survive this climate. It is almost August, the peak of summer, but the temperature dips into the low forties at night and that is winter to our bodies. I also make a mental note to look around for more blankets for our bed.

Stubby falls in and begins leading us to the cabin. His curly matted red and white hair, long, knobby legs and large, inquisitive eyes bring a huge smile to my face and warmth to my heart. This kind of simple joy is a feeling so foreign, so long forgotten, but so welcome that it brings tears to my eyes. The muscles that are pulling the corners of my mouth upward simultaneously tug on my heart, pulling it up from where it has been lying low, and instantly my spirits are lifted. I feel better than I have in weeks.

Morning fog is rising from the ground; an otherworldly, gauzy moisture lightly kissing our faces. My muscles are warming, my joints are loosening, my spirits are lifting and it occurs to me what a beautiful place this is. I am struck by the unbelievable greenness of the grass and the blueness of the sky. There is a malleable sense of stillness and peace that seems to be oozing from the ground. The sights, the sounds, the colors all caress me, embrace me and stir within me a welcome sense of belonging.

After breakfast, but before I tackle the mountain of dirty dishes, Wayne shows me how to mix the dry formula for Stubby's morning bottle. This huge plastic thing is like no baby bottle I have ever seen. The nipple alone is longer and bigger around than a grown man's thumb, and the bottle it screws on to is the size of one of those big plastic cups you get when you order a glass of iced tea in a Texas restaurant. It takes two hands and real stamina to feed Stubby. He attacks the bottle with so much gusto that he almost knocks me down before I am able to back myself up against the outside wall of the log cabin for support, laughing for the first time since I can remember.

The precious little knobby-kneed calf begins following me around whenever I come outside the cabin during the day. He nudges against my legs and lets out a sweet cry trying to convince me it's feeding time. I bend down to pat him on his side, talk sweet to him for a moment and head off to the laundry room or the woodpile, or wherever my chores are taking me. He follows close behind for a while, then something more interesting catches his attention and he's gone to find trouble. Feeding Stubby is one chore I look forward to twice a day. Like clockwork every morning around 7:00 and every evening around 5:00, Stubby makes his way to the cabin and sings his feed-me song as he paces around in circles beside the steps of the front porch. And when he sees me coming down the steps with that huge bottle in my hands he lumbers toward me with what I believe is a smile on his little cow face.

That first night on the farm, after a wonderful dinner of pan-fried salmon steaks seasoned with salt, lemon and paprika, fried diced potatoes sprinkled with garlic salt, and fresh broccoli from the green house; while everyone sits around the table, full and satisfied, praising me for the wonderful meal, I begin to clear the table and stack the dishes in the sink. It has been a great day. Shane and I are out of the cold, empty apartment and the hungry weekend is over. We've got plenty of food to eat, a place to sleep and we're with good people in a warm kitchen. I begin to relax for the first time in forever. My shoulders have lowered several inches, my stomach is full and satisfied, and my mind is clear. There are unasked questions hanging in the air but the mood is easy. Perhaps Wayne has warned the children not to be nosy. The conversation is light and impersonal and I am happy. I must be careful to call my husband Roy, but things are definitely looking up. It is nice to be appreciated and needed. I would cook every day for the rest of my life if it could always be like this.

Suddenly, Wayne and the children are screaming at me.

What are you doing? Stop! Turn it off! You're wasting water!

The water had been running down the drain as I rinsed off the dishes, stacking them on the counter in preparation to be washed in a sink-full of clean, soapy water; the way I've done dishes all my life; the way I learned as soon as I was big enough to reach the sink standing on a kitchen chair. Jillian comes over and shows me how to wash dishes in a place where the water comes from a well with a pump that sometimes runs dry, or gets so low it can't be pumped, or something else I don't understand. I don't want to do anything that might make them send me away so I quickly adapt to running one sink-full of soapy water to wash the dishes in, and one sink-full of clean water to rinse the dishes in. By the time I'm finished, the soapy water is very dirty and the rinse water is very soapy, but the dishes are done.

Shane and I are allowed to take showers that night, but are warned that we won't get another one for a week. I get used to washing dishes the Alaska way, but I never get used to only getting one shower a week. Wayne and the kids have their shower times, apparently during the weeknights after Shane and I retire to the fifth-wheel trailer. Shane gets into the habit of taking his shower on Saturday nights after supper, and I enjoy mine on Friday mornings after breakfast. It is an onerous, uphill battle each week waiting for the sweet relief of the hot water and soap to wash away the dirt, sweat, tension and hard work of six days on the ranch. A warm, wet washcloth here and there through the week just doesn't compare. There are a few times when I just can't go all week without shampooing my greasy hair and I cheat. Some afternoons when everyone else is out working, I quickly wash my hair with dish soap in the kitchen sink, towel it as dry as I can get it, then pull it back into a ponytail hoping no one will notice.

One day I get the opportunity to go into town with a wonderful neighbor I remember only as Mrs. K. She and her husband are retired and live at the end of the road near the mailboxes. She introduces herself to me one pretty day we both are checking for mail at the same time. She is an angel of a lady, all warm and rosy and she invites me over for a piece of pie. I say no, that I really need to get back, but she insists and before I know it I'm sitting in her warm kitchen sipping hot tea from a heavy mug and eating a piece of rhubarb custard pie. Her husband, Mr. K., sits across the large open room in a leather recliner working a crossword puzzle, looking up and smiling at me every few minutes; a radio plays some talk show and I learn that it is an NPR station. I find it very interesting and make a mental note to listen again someday. Mrs. K. sits across the table from me bouncing her tea bag in and out of her mug, a nice smile on her face. Her voice is old but smooth like velvet and when she speaks, which is just the right amount. I'm comfortable in her presence. She tells me a little about the town of Homer, the fishing families down the road, the young couple around the corner that just finished building their own log cabin. They'll be starting a family of their own soon she says. Occasionally, she asks me something about myself. Her questions catch me off guard. She can tell and doesn't push when I don't find the words to answer her. She just smiles and wipes her soft hands on the dishtowel she's holding in her lap. I finish the pie and tell her it's the best pie I've ever tasted, because it is, and she gets out paper and a pen and writes down the recipe for me. I fold the piece of paper and put it into the kangaroo pocket on the front of the gray pullover sweatshirt I'm wearing that used to be Jillian's.

Soon we are outside where Mrs. K is showing me her wonderful yard and garden full of vibrant-colored flowers and I know I will never remember the names she gives them. That's when I spot the tree swing. It's the tallest swing I've ever seen in my life. The ropes are at least twenty feet long and are attached to a huge branch of a very tall tree. Mrs. K. sees me admiring it and tells me the name of the tree too. A 2" X 6" piece of wood, worn smooth by years of use, serves as the seat of the swing. Mrs. K. says I must try it. Oh no, I couldn't. But she is persuasive and the next instant I am sitting on the swing and I'm six years old again; but this time my mother is Mrs. K. and no one gets drunk, there is never any yelling or fighting at night, and there is always pie after school. I pump my legs as hard as I can and I am flying! The ground beneath me disappears on the forward arc as the yard slopes off into a deep ravine, and I'm so high up on the backward arc that the sky swallows me and I catch a glimpse of the sparkling water of the bay just before I'm swooping down again. When I say good-bye Mrs. K. gives me a soft hug and says I am welcome to come over any time.

A few days later Mrs. K. comes to get me and takes me to town. She and Wayne must have talked on the phone. Wayne gives me some cash to pick up a few things that are needed around the house and says to spend what is left on myself. We drive to a church and park in the rear. Mrs. K. has a key and we go inside through a metal side door. She says she runs the thrift store for the church and why don't I pick out a few things for Roy and myself, no charge.

That sweatshirt won't keep you warm all winter, she says.

There's so much to choose from but I don't want to be greedy and I don't know where to start. Mrs. K. picks up a slate blue sweater and holds it up to me. She says it's a good color for me and throws it across her forearm. I try on a couple pairs of jeans and she throws them across her forearm too and smiles and nods. There are socks and gloves and thermal underwear, and I don't like the idea of wearing someone's used underwear, but I don't like being cold even more, so we add those to the growing pile across Mrs. K's arm and she just keeps smiling. I find a few things for Shane, and when we're finished, she finds a green army duffle bag and we stuff it full of our new clothes and lock the church door behind us.

Mrs. K. buys us lunch at McDonalds, and at an artsy little book/gift shop next door to a travel agency, she encourages me to buy the journal I have picked up and am running my fingers over. The cover is turquoise fabric with a Japanese pagoda garden scene and I open the book to look inside even though I know its pages are empty.

That night I write my first entry:

September 26, 1985

Mrs. K drove me into town for some shopping and lunch today and despite the cold, constant drizzle of rain, I really enjoyed myself. I found several things we needed for the impending winter months. Thermals, hats, pants, wool shirts and gloves. I spent $4.95 today, and that went for this book I'm writing in now. All of the clothes came from a thrift store owned by a church that Mrs. K helps operate. I thank the Lord for people like Mrs. K. I'm not feeling well this *evening. I hope I didn't overdo my first day out in six weeks.*

Chapter Fifteen

My days are full and my nights are quiet. I finally have a purposeful and neat life but deep down I know it can't last. I am usually able to keep busy enough to push my dark secrets to the background. Some days though, I wonder about what's going on back home and my heart hurts. Those are the days I fight back tears of homesickness and worry.

There is a sense of purpose and a welcome routine to my kitchen duties. Everyone loves my cooking and I myself am in awe of the meals I continue to put on the table. Feeding people makes me feel important.

There are two stoves in the kitchen, one is electric and one runs on propane gas. The electric stove has one top burner that works and the oven works, but it doesn't have a thermostat so it's 500 degrees or nothing. The propane stove is barely 20 inches wide and the top burners work, but you have to strike a match to light the oven and that scares me, so I don't use it.

I make do by baking everything in the electric oven that only knows 500 degrees. To keep the food from burning, I prop open the oven door with different sized blocks of wood. Every day is a miracle because everything I cook turns out perfectly. Everyone raves about how delicious the casseroles are. How moist and tender the round steak is, and how flaky and tender the piecrusts are. Nothing burns. Nothing is half-cooked.

When I'm not doing huge piles of laundry, stocking the wood supply at the main cabin and at the trailer, or washing dishes, I can usually be found in the kitchen baking or cooking. Wayne shows me how to mix up the bread dough, let it rise, knead it, and let it rise again in the pans before baking them.

Fill this small saucepan half full of water and heat it on the stove until just before it starts boiling. Stir in two of these packets of yeast and let it sit. See the little bubbles all on top? That's how you know it's alive, he says. Then he gets out the biggest mixing bowl I've ever seen and scoops four large handfuls of flour from the sack under the counter and throws them into the bowl. After that, he takes the salt and shakes it over the flour in the bowl for about 10 seconds. Next he adds two large pinches of sugar, and then he pours in the yeast mixture. He tells me to take the wooden spoon and mix all that up real good. I start stirring while he grabs the big jug of oil. As I stir, he slowly pours in the oil. I stir and he pours. I stir and he pours. I stir and stir and stir and he adds more flour, a little at a time. Just when I think the wooden spoon will break, and I can't stir any more, he says it's ready to work. He sprinkles some flour onto the counter top, takes the lump of dough out of the bowl and begins kneading it. He gathers the dough into a ball and folds it in half toward his body, presses down and out, turns it, then folds and presses, gathers, turns, folds and presses for about ten minutes, until the blob of dough has the look and feel of smooth elastic. While he does that he has me wash, rinse and grease the same large mixing bowl. He places the dough into the bowl rolling it around so that the whole ball is shiny with the grease I coated the inside of the bowl with. Then we cover the bowl with a towel and set it on the coffee table in the living room near the fireplace. When we go to check on it about an hour later, I can't believe my eyes. The dough has more than doubled in size! It seems alive. The towel we had covered it with looks like a tiny scrap of material lost on top of a mountain. Wayne removes the towel and punches his fist into the center of the dough, leaving an imprint of his knuckles. We take the bowl back into the kitchen and prepare the six loaf pans by greasing them with more oil. Wayne pours a quick splash into each pan, then takes one at a time and rolls it around until the oil covers all four sides as well as the bottom.

You tear off a hunk about this big (Wayne holds up a glob of dough that just fills his large hand, showing me) and you work it like before, but only once or twice this time. Then you shape it like so. He flattens it out, then rolls the sides in and pinches it here and there. After all six pans are filled with chunks of dough we cover them with more towels and let them sit on the kitchen counter to rise again. After another hour or so, they are ready to put into the oven two at a time. On bread-baking day, the last of the loaves are usually still baking when the gang shows up for lunch. The house is filled with the unmistakable aroma of fresh-baked bread. We eat leftover soup and warm bread, or potted meat sandwiches on those days, enjoying the warm kitchen and its comforting aromas.

I bake six loaves of bread every other day from the first of August through the end of October when we leave Homer for good. We eat one loaf at breakfast, one at lunch and another loaf for supper every day. A slice of bread with jam is a delicious afternoon snack. The days I don't bake bread, I bake a cake or a couple of pies. There is a piecrust recipe scribbled in pencil on the back of an envelope that I find in the junk drawer in the kitchen. That piecrust comes out light and flaky every time. It amazes me daily that the right mix of the simplest ingredients, combined with the perfect oven temperature, transforms into mouth-watering food that both satisfies and nourishes our bodies.

For weeks, everyone's favorite is Mrs. K's rhubarb custard pie. Rhubarb grows in large, random clusters around the yard. One day while Jillian and I are carrying huge bundles of laundry to the Quonset hut where the washing machine is I ask what is that plant over there? She tells me it is rhubarb. It looks like celery but is red like a pomegranate and has long, narrow green and red leaves. Once again I am in awe; this time over the fact that everyone loves rhubarb and here it is, growing wild all over the place!

If I'm not baking pies and cakes, or kneading bread dough, I am throwing together a casserole or pan-frying salmon steaks or fresh halibut and there are always potatoes to peel or bake. There are several jars of herbs and spices lined up on the back of the stove and I find myself grabbing one, then another and fearlessly flavoring everything. Everything is delicious. Nothing is too spicy, never too much salt. Those angels keep whispering and I keep doing what they tell me. They tell me everything; when to grab the oregano, what to put lemon on, where to use the bay leaves, and how much paprika is enough.

There are no pauses in my motions, no hesitations. With the angels guiding me, I am a bold, confident cook.

But I'm not always in the kitchen.

On the days I don't bake the bread, the time between doing the breakfast dishes and starting lunch is my favorite time of day because those precious hours are mine. The kids are out with the men cutting firewood, building a new barn, working on the hay baler, filling troughs with feed, mending fence, or any number of other chores. I spend that time wandering the grounds around the log cabin. I discover the huge strawberry patch where I eat as many of the giant, juicy red berries as I take back to the kitchen. I explore the humid greenhouse where broccoli, cauliflower, tomatoes, onions, cabbage, beans, corn and more grow larger than life in waist-high beds filled with fertile dirt. There are musty barns to explore, families of horses to greet and talk to, and a long walk down a dirt road to the mailbox that I gladly add to my list of chores.

Later, I get brave and venture into the woods north of the cabin where I discover a whole new world. The floor of the forest is covered in a plush, carpet-like moss and it takes getting used to walking on because you sink several inches with each step. It kind of reminds me of walking on a sandy beach, it takes effort. The canopy of trees overhead is so thick that only bits and pieces of blue sky can be seen overhead. Narrow rays of sunshine slice their way between the tree branches; slanted silver swords lighting my way. The fresh, pungent summer smells of the forest bring me home to the natural, forgotten spiritual place deep inside me. The part of me where hope lives, where prayers are answered and life feels good. I breathe in the intoxicating aromas of the ancient earth and the greenest moss and the towering trees and the sweetest berries and the beautiful flowers with their faces turned toward heaven, and the multitude of musky fungi. It is a healing tonic, a powerful perfume that swims through me and stirs my soul back to life with such force and certainty that it moves me to my knees. There in the presence of the trees, I put my forehead against the plush mossy floor of the forest and weep like a baby. And later, when the tears begin to dry, I pour out my heart praying fervently to God who is the same yesterday, today and tomorrow; thankful for this place, these people, the opportunity of peace and health. And that day I am made new.

Each day I discover something more awesome and majestic than what I found the day before. I treasure my lone journeys into the woods, up the side of the mountain, down toward the road to town. Never have I experienced such peace and solitude. There are no cars, no houses; no people. It is all mine and I savor the precious gift of every sight, every sound; every fragrance.

As the days go by I venture deeper and deeper into the woods. I want to see everything; experience the joy of every perfect flower petal, be moved to tears by the silence broken only by the leaves swaying on a gentle breeze. My morning walks keep me grounded. The woods are my sanctuary, each footstep a meditation in movement. I fiercely protect my time alone and become selfish, wanting to keep it all to myself.

One day, while walking deep in the woods, I come upon a mushroom growing at the base of a giant tree. There are mushrooms everywhere; some big, some small, some colorful, some white, some earthy brown, and some growing in places you'd never imagine, but there are no other mushrooms like this one. This mushroom is the deep purple color of grape Kool-Aid and is the size of a Frisbee standing about eight inches high on a stem as big around as a rolling pin. There is a slice of sunlight shining right down on top of its cap making it shine like a huge grape gum drop waiting to be plucked up by the hand of a giant. I try to burn the image in my mind forever, taking pictures of it with my mind by holding my eyes open for several seconds, then closing them for even longer, holding them open then closing them over and over again.

On these walks, I have caught glimpses of furry creatures that I do not know the names of; I have seen a bald eagle silently gliding on one invisible air current after another and I write about them in my new journal.

And one day I see a bear! He is standing on his hind legs, facing my direction, about a hundred yards away. The morning is cool and clear and white puffs of cottony clouds dot the deep blue sky. Everything glistens in the sunlight as if washed clean by the previous night's gentle rain. Puddles of rainwater on the road reflect the deep blue of the sky giving the impression that random sized bits of the sky have been placed gently on the road, bringing heaven down to earth. I am wearing large rubber boots over my own work boots with the thick wool insoles. Several mismatched pairs of these rubber boots, in a variety of sizes, and some lonely lefts and rights can always be found on the large front porch of the log cabin. It rains a minimum of three times a week for several hours and most of the yard is dirt, the driveway is dirt, and the road leading to town is dirt. All that rain on all that dirt makes for a ton of mud that everyone makes a concerted effort to keep out of the house. Slipping on a pair of rubber boots becomes second nature when I leave the house. Often I am lucky enough to find a pair not so large that they flop around clown-like with each slippery step. Walking in a good pair takes practice. Running is out of the question. I'm taking a walk up the side of Bald Mountain behind the cabin, and have left the dirt road that circles the perimeter of the house.

I am strolling through the tall grass that is chest high, holding my arms out like wings and letting the tips of the grass tickle the palms of my hands. I am completely lost in the moment, enjoying the magic of the day with child-like abandon when something makes me stop and take in the larger picture. To the south, beyond the cabin and the woods that separates it from the paved road to town, is the marvelously blue water lapping on the shores of Kachemack Bay, and beyond it, the snow-capped mountains on Kodiak Island. To my left, the sea of tall, green grass swaying in the breeze continues for as far as I can see. About a mile in the distance the shiny tin roof of a small cabin glitters like a diamond. And when I turn to my right, there he is, about a hundred yards away, standing in a clearing where the telephone lines run up the adjacent hill. We study each other in the stillness between a single breath that lasts a lifetime.

A detached fragment of time, dislodged, floating, full and rich, a Polaroid snapshot unbound by gravity. And then I blink. In that instant, the snapshot clicks into its place in the world and time begins again, the earth once more turns on its axis and I exhale.

I calculate how far away from the cabin I am, stealing a quick glance toward the house then back to the bear. I consider fate and say a prayer. My eyes stay on him but my feet begin moving me slowly toward the cabin, the tall grass lying down beneath the soles of my rubber boots. When I reach the road, thirty yards from the cabin, he drops down on all fours and moves in my direction. As my hand reaches for and finds the handle of the screen door on the back porch I turn and see the imposing brown bear, now only fifty yards away, stop, roll his head making a circle with his nose, then turn and go down on all fours. I want to believe that he just wanted to say hi, and would not have hurt me as I stand behind the screen door watching him amble back up the side of the hill, my heartbeat slowing.

I never see another bear the whole time we're there but we do eat bear meat one night for supper. A neighbor had gone bear hunting and gives Wayne a huge 'ham'. I lightly salt and pepper it, coat it with flour and braise it in oil, put it in a roasting pan with some water and a chopped onion, sprinkle it with chives and cook it in the electric oven for three hours, using the one inch thick chunk of wood to prop open the oven door. I steam some fresh broccoli and cauliflower, open a can of carrots, put them in a saucepan with half a cup of orange juice and a dash of ginger, fry some diced potatoes, set out the bread and jam and we all sit down for supper. Quickly, someone gets up and grabs the mustard from the refrigerator as the meat still has a very strong, gamey flavor. I try dousing mine in mustard too, but still it is too strong for me. Shane finishes off my slice of bear meat and I fill up on vegetables.

September 29, 1985

The wind blew so hard last night that it blew down our stovepipe from the roof of the mudroom. Trees are down everywhere. One fell on the power lines, and we've had no electricity since early this morning. I've never cooked a whole meal on a wood stove before, but I may tonight.

There have been several firsts for me up here: herding cattle, picking strawberries, hauling wood and hay, eating moose and rhubarb, running (slowly) from a bear and touching a glacier are just a few.

They say this has been an unusually cold summer. The highest temp I've seen in this area was sixty degrees; and that was in August. I hope it's not a sign for an extremely cold winter. I'm cold already.

The sun shows less each day. They say that soon it will be getting light at 10:00 am and getting dark at 4:30 pm.

So much wholesome exercise, honest labor and back-to-basics living has a way of grounding lost souls; bringing us back to nature, back to God. God is everywhere: in the ground, in the trees, in the rainbows that sometimes seem to begin on a spot of ground right outside the kitchen door, and in the food I miraculously prepare to perfection day in and day out. I am new again, and even Shane is softer and gentler, easier to be around. We are thriving.

I catch myself watching Shane one day as we unload another pile of wood from the flatbed trailer. We are stacking it outside our mudroom so we can split it and it will be ready to take inside to burn. Wayne lets us borrow the gas splitter, which makes the job go much quicker. The wood-burning stove is our only source of heat and each night seems colder than the last. We don't want to take the chance of running out of wood, so when there is time, Shane and I go to the woods, find and cut up fallen trees with a chainsaw, load the manageable pieces onto the flatbed, drive to the trailer, unload and stack it, and then split it into quarters for burning. I had heard it said that firewood warms you three or four times before you ever burn it. Now I understand what that means. I have sweated over this wood four times already just to get it here. It is late afternoon on a warm, sunny day. Soon, the sun will disappear and night will bring its own wonders. We have been working in the hay fields all day. We eat cold sandwiches out in the fields for lunch and supper that I make early in the morning. There are stretches of three and four days like this where we live and breathe hay. The hay is feed for the cattle and in order to have enough to make it through the cold winter months, the barns must all be full. Bringing in the hay is top priority on a cattle ranch, and no one is excluded from the backbreaking labor of bringing it in. We are lucky if we get three days in a row without rain so if the sun is shining, we are in the fields. For about four weeks we are all either loading bales of hay onto a truck, unloading bales of hay from a truck, or stacking bales of hay in a barn. During that time we have extra help. I'm never sure how many we'll have for each meal, but whoever shows up gets fed, so I start making extra food just in case. The angels tell me how much more meat to thaw and how many more potatoes to peel and it is always just the right amount.

Bringing in hay is the dirtiest job I've ever done. At the end of those long, hard days there is hay or the dust of hay all over my clothes, in my hair, in my ears, and in my nose. At night I take off my clothes and find hay dust inside my bra, in my underwear and between my toes.

After a couple days of throwing those 70 pound bales up over my head, my back goes out and I earn the prized job of driving the truck around the field while the others load the bales onto the flat-bed trailer and someone else stacks them five and six high until it is full and someone whistles and I drive us back to the barns where it is unloaded and we head out again. After the first couple days of this I am praying for rain just to get a break, to get back into the kitchen and cook again. I need to bake the bread. Everyone is ready for a hot and hearty meal after working so hard. And the rain always comes; leaving behind multiple ribbons of vibrant rainbows we all admire and struggle to find words to describe.

Shane and I are both filthy and exhausted from working the hay and cutting the wood. Shane has discarded his shirt and is standing up on the flatbed. As I watch him lift one huge log after another, tossing them to the ground, I catch a glimpse of the man I fell in love with; not the stoned man I married, not the mad man I have lived with for seven years, not the man with pasty skin and sunken eyes, so paranoid and strung out on downers that he sleeps with a gun under his pillow; but the strong, confident man who knows himself, who can smile at me and sweep me off my feet. This is the man I danced with at Spencer's Corner a lifetime ago, the man with charm and charisma. I marvel at his strength, at the length and firmness of his muscular arms and back. He wears on his face a scruffy, sexy 3-day beard, his sun-streaked hair is short and shaggy and his jeans are fitting snuggly to his legs that are filling out. This is the man I have missed and mourned. This is the man I want to share my life with. Could I? Would I stay here in Alaska with my husband and carve out a new life? Would we have the children I've longed for and raise them in a log cabin of our own, living off the land just like Shane always wanted to? We could home school our kids and they would be healthy and happy, running barefoot through the cool grass by day and sleeping snug by the fire at night. They would never know the life we left behind.

The life we left behind. Oh God. Will the life we left behind catch up with us?

Shane catches me watching him and flashes me his sexy smile. I see the twinkle in his eyes that has been missing for so long and it makes me sad. I know, deep down, with a crystal-clear certainty that we will never live the dream. It is a mirage, a bright and shining jewel forever out of my reach. Even on my tippy-toes, with my long arms stretched to their limit and leaning to the point of no return, I cannot reach that dream and make it my own.

Chapter Sixteen

October 10, 1985
The Northern Lights put on a fantastic light show last weekend. It was another first for me, and just one of many glimpses into God's magnificence that I've experienced here. They were mostly lime green with an occasional reddish pink one dancing across the sky, west to east, growing taller and brighter and brighter, then shrinking and slowly fading away. We stood outside with the frosty ground beneath our feet and the magic in the sky until our teeth chattered and we had to come indoors. Snug in bed, with a cozy fire burning in the stove, I fell asleep wondering how these incredible, unexplained light shows existed and I had never even heard of them before.

As the Alaskan days grow shorter, colder and darker, I spend more and more time indoors where my thoughts turn inward. I write in my journal, careful not to mention names or divulge any secrets that will give us away.

August turns into September; September fades into October and there is more and more free time as the hay is safely stored in the barns, the fences mended and the ranch has been readied for the season that separates the boys from the men. I am homesick and not looking forward to a long, dark winter. I am cold all the time, my body is hurting, I am feeling sick and I really miss my family. I spend hours lying awake with my eyes shut, watching the movie of my life play in my mind like bits of film pieced together in an editing room. Similar scenes, experienced years apart, find each other and store themselves together in the same file drawer in my brain. After experiencing the northern lights, the memory of it finds its way to the file drawer where my strangest personal experiences live. I find the northern lights tucked snuggly in between my out-of-body experience and the time I ate magic mushrooms.

My out-of-body experience happens in a dentist's chair and is brought on by laughing gas while I'm having my wisdom teeth removed. I am nineteen years old. The dentist has given me Valium so I will relax. He has shot my gums full of Novocain and he has strapped to my face a small gas mask that only covers my nose, reminding me that if I start feeling uncomfortable I can simply take a couple of breaths through my mouth and the feeling will go away.

Almost immediately after inhaling the gas I float out of my body and can see myself lying in the chair; see the dentist perched on his squatty stool nearby, preparing to go to work in my mouth. Then I am outside. I have floated beyond the building and can see rooftops, treetops and roads with their undulating rows of multi-colored vehicles, and they look to me like strings of colorful beads. A part of me wants to pick up the string and send the beads scattering and splashing into the backyard swimming pools of the houses penned in by six-foot privacy fences. As I continue floating upward, I see how our beautiful earth has been carved into surveyable sections of land, patchwork plots; deep, deliberate scars reducing the land into tiny pieces with owners names recorded as volumes and page numbers in official city record books.

Soon I am so high in the sky that the scars on the surface of the land are faded and there is only blue and green and I can see the curvature of the earth. Now I am in deep dark space and our planet is just a blue glow far in the distance and that's when I begin to worry that I might not be able to find my way back to my body. And I panic. I draw in a deep breath through my mouth and instantly I am back and I never left and the world feels so small. The dentist gives me a little smile and tells me I'm doing fine.

But the thing that takes up the most space in that file drawer in my brain is my night of clear thoughts and intuitive understanding sometime in 1981 when Shane and I eat sugar cubes laced with psilocybin, or magic mushrooms.

My trip begins with a fit of uncontrollable laughter, in our car, almost two hours after eating the sugar cubes. Shane and I have been at the house of some friends and decide to drive home. Since so much time has passed and nothing has happened, Shane thinks the magic mushrooms are duds. It makes me think of fireworks bought from a roadside stand; colorful wrappers promising big bangs and bright bursts of light but when you get them home they die one disappointing fizzle, hiss and pop after another. Duds. But he is wrong. There is some magic in these mushrooms after all.

It's a warm spring night and we have removed the T-tops from our sporty brown Cutlass Salon and have tucked them safely into the trunk. Shane is driving. The radio is on. The warm night air caresses our faces and our young, thin, bare arms. It is late and I am tired. I'm sitting in the passenger seat with my head back and my eyes closed just wanting to get home and go to bed. We smoked a few joints at Tommy and Jane's house. I am very relaxed.

Tommy is missing the ends of his index and middle fingers on his right hand and I like to watch him roll joints. With practiced finesse he rolls the tightest, thinnest joints of anyone I know. Shane always rolls his too thick. People laugh and joke about Cheech and Chong when Shane rolls one and hands it to them for the first time. No matter how good the pot is Shane rolls them full and round giving him something he can hold on to and really get his lips around, he says with a sexy smile before putting the joint between his lips and setting the end of it on fire. Tommy's thin but firm joints are elegant and refined and he only uses half the paper. After first seeing him roll one joint, I begin fashioning mine just like his and get pretty good at it. Shane doesn't like them much but he still smokes them.

We come to a stop light and I open one eye just enough to see a smeary yellow light turn red. KZEW, Texas' Best Rock is cranked up on the radio. High from the pot and tired from another long day of doing nothing, the music ends and I hear the DJ say something I find hysterical. My eyes fly open, I burst out laughing, sit up on the edge of my seat and grab Shane's forearm asking if he had just heard this thing that I think is the funniest thing in the world. But I can't talk, I'm laughing so hard. And then Shane is laughing too. And I don't know if he has heard what I just heard or if my laughter is so contagious that he has been infected, because each time I try to repeat the funny thing, my laugh fills me up again and renders me speechless. We share this long laugh for an eternity and each time our eyes meet, the laughter grows another arm or leg until it is an octopus embracing us eight different ways, tickling every funny bone in our bodies, reminding us we are alive and young and free and having fun and we are teetering on the edge of the high dive, riding the roller coaster up, up, up to the summit, the precipice, the point of no return. And it's then that I know I am going to fall. I am going to fall and I have no idea where I will land.

Shane's laughter slows and trickles and trails off as composure takes hold. Mine doesn't slow down. My sides are aching. I can't catch my breath and I think ever so quickly; the lightning-fast way your brain will do, taking you from one corner of the universe to another in the blink of an eye, that surely this is how I will die. Bouncing now from thoughts of death to birth to love to war to babies' tiny fat little toes to grandma's wrinkles to Mars and Venus and back to death again, my trip has begun. With my arms wrapped around my middle in an attempt to keep my insides from escaping and my eyes clinched shut, tears stream down my face as I roll out of my seat and down into the floorboard. My knees are on the scratchy carpet where a grain of dirt is digging into my right knee bringing to mind the Princess and the Pea. With my feet kicking and my fists now pounding into the tan vinyl upholstery, I laugh the laughter of supreme release; a release previously unknown to me, a release with no limits, no boundaries and no words. The magic mushrooms have taken me there.

My hysterical laughter is escaping our car and drawing curious attention and tentative smiles from sober passengers in nearby vehicles. Shane pulls me by both shoulders back into my seat, grabs my chin and forces me to look into his eyes that are speaking volumes.

Be cool, baby! He whispers gently, releasing his grip on my chin and smoothing my blond hair with his slow hand. You're losing it.

My body first, then my mind find themselves together once more in this world. The maniacal laughter has stopped, leaving me dog paddling in its wide wake. I draw in a deep, much-needed breath of fresh air and nod to Shane as I settle back into my seat, unable to bring words to my mouth. The light turns green and I watch suspiciously as the green bulb melts into a long smeary streak that follows our left turn. All lights follow suit; street lights, head lights, neon signs, every light in the world is melting into a molten blob as we pass them and each one takes on a new, random shape willed to it at the suggestion of my altered mind. The luminous orbs of my new world melt and morph and merge with the first green light and continue to follow us home; a sensual, living rainbow propelled forward by the seeming promise of casual merrymaking. George Thorogood is singing *Bad To The Bone* and I see fire hot musical notes jumping from the speakers on the dashboard, crashing into the windshield and sliding up and out the open roof of the car. Unencumbered by gravity, they rise into the air uniting with the rainbow, bringing to the union the unbridled dimension of sound.

Now I am home, in my own bathroom puking up my guts. Tiny three-headed purple and orange demons, their red eyes glowing, black slimy worms with multiple arms, and all the evil inside me comes pouring from my mouth and splashes into the toilet. In wide-eyed terror, I flush the toilet quickly and watch them disappear, to hell? I think briefly. At the sink, I rinse out my mouth, splash cool water on my face and look into the mirror. It is impossible to see my face through all the color and movement in the air between the mirror and me. What is all this stuff? I reach for it but it darts away like mercury at the threat of my touch. I'm suddenly shivering in my t-shirt and bare feet and Shane is helping me into the warm comfort of the heated waterbed and I pull the covers up to my chin. The wavy motion sets off a whole new series of doors in my mind opening and closing and dancing around concepts and ideas and thoughts; what I sense are combinations to secret locks and formulas for the true meaning of life.

I am riding a roller coaster in my mind that knows no boundaries and is not limited to the laws and dimensions of this world. Up, down, left, right, and diagonally, all at the same time, I move through invisible folds in time. With each peak and valley I comprehend another wealth of information, gain new wisdom, fresh perspectives; new clarity. I see brilliance, discern grace and perceive humanity. I turn and put my hand on the cool, dry wall beside the bed and my hand goes through it and comes out the other side and I am on the other side to greet it. There is music in the living room. The words and the melodies are escaping the constricted caverns of the huge speakers and they are coming purposefully down the hallway and into the bedroom where, lying on the bed I can see them even with my eyes closed. I see my body get up and dance with them but I do not move.

My journey continues; I am ebbing and flowing, rising and swelling and ebbing and flowing and rising and rising and rising until, in a brilliant crescendo, I crash into the only thing that is real.

And it is love.

And love is not a word or an idea or even a place to go to or a thing to strive for. It is not something to grasp and smother and mold and change. It cannot be orchestrated, played, controlled or manipulated. You cannot cup it tenderly in your open hand or wish it into being through fervent prayer.

But you can crash into it, head on and when you do, you are home. And when you're home, that's what matters.

I am embraced by this pure, warm, deep world of love and it takes me through tunnels and curves and twists and turns of joyous rapture and together (because now we are one) we explode through to a place where there is no distinction between my body and any world. Pure light comes into and fills me without first being filtered through my human consciousness, assumptions and expectations. It is not about me. It is not about anyone. It just is. And it is love and love is everything. And I know without knowing that I will be different after this.

Several lifetimes pass. And then Shane is telling me to get up. We're going fishing.

Sitting on a wooden pier with a fishing pole in my hand, I'm staring into the muddy water of a lake. I do not remember getting here. The sun is just rising and all around me this world is emerging from the cocoon of darkness. Little bits of sunshine are getting trapped inside drops of dew and the ground is covered in liquid diamonds. The sky is my canvas and when I wave my hand across the horizon the wispy clouds reluctantly follow my command, stretching and bending at my will, but then they snap back into their rightful places standing attention to some greater authority.

As soon as I perceive it, as soon as I think it, it is true. The magic is wearing off. I feel it all slipping away, going to the place where misplaced keys and lost friends dwell. The magnetic pull of this earth and its corresponding laws are beginning to thwart the effect of the remaining magic of the mushrooms, and an imperceptible re-aligning of the molecules has begun. I panic at the thought of losing all I have learned, of forgetting what is important, of misplacing the truth, of losing love. All the pieces of the puzzle had found a home and now they are floating away, ethereal memories slipping back to the place where dreams go to live at first light, running from the grasp of your wakened mind.

I want desperately to remember where the

pieces go so the next time everything falls apart I have a defense; I have knowledge and words of ammunition. But the full magnitude and power of my experience can already call itself a memory. In a panic not to lose it all, I close my eyes and concentrate. And that's when I find the fish. There are several just under the pier where we sit. There is one huge fish about twenty yards out at ten o'clock. Another small school swims past between me and where my line disappears into the water, all of them ignoring my bait. I can't see them but I know they are there. I can feel them.

And I smile. It is a gift, one last glimpse into the invisible world; the place our minds can go only when they are free of being filtered through the sieve of human assumptions and expectations.

The sun is high in the sky when we pull our lines out of the water and go home to crash. And when I wake up the next morning (eighteen hours later) I stand under the hot water of the shower for what seems like weeks, running my hands over and over my shampooed head just to hear the squeak of clean, contemplating love.

Chapter Seventeen

October 12, 1985
Today was the first day in seven that I didn't
get sick. I keep thinking I might be pregnant, but
then something tells me I'm not. Time will tell. We
bought our airline tickets for home today.

We've been in Alaska since mid-July. Gone are the bright sunny days and the darkless nights. Gone are the solitary walks through the woods and my alone time. I'm sick to my stomach and throw up before and after every meal. I've begun keeping a packet of saltines beside the bed for first thing in the morning. It takes all the strength and will I possess to force myself into the kitchen. The thought of food turns my stomach. The sight of food turns my stomach. Mornings are the worst and the eggs do me in every day. Cracking eight or ten of them into a bowl for scrambling, the slimy translucence of the white part sends me to the bathroom before I can get them into the iron skillet. It feels like I've been sick for months. I can't remember when I felt good. All the signs are pointing toward it, but in the light of day I won't even let myself think I might be pregnant. Not now. Not when I'm three thousand miles from home hiding from the law without a dime to my name. Not when I'm convinced I must divorce Shane and start my life over.

But there are weak moments of mommy hope that slip through the armor of my mind when I let myself feel pregnant and think maybe, just maybe... Every fiber of my being knows I'm meant to be a mommy and sometimes my arms ache to hold and caress my baby. But not now.

I've definitely been putting on some weight and my breasts are getting huge. And then the words of two different doctors from over the years come crashing down on my tender hope.

So in the light of day I tell myself it's just a bug and remember that it's not unusual for me to skip my period; some years I only have three or four. It's no big deal. I'm not pregnant. I can't be pregnant.

But late at night, I'm haunted by Shane's incisive words spoken to me inside our trailer shortly after our arrival at the ranch.

I--just-gave—-you-a—-ba-by-girl, he rasped into my ear before rolling his sweaty body off me.

I lie awake long after his breathing has slowed and the rhythm of sleep settles him, cupping my naked belly with both my hands, wondering if he could really know such a thing - wondering which spooks me more, his haunting words, or my aching wish to make them come true. So I spend my days denying it, and my nights feeling more and more sure of what I hope for.

I barely have enough clothes to keep from freezing. I sleep with my head covered; curled up next to Shane in my long johns underneath a sheet, a wool army blanket, a cotton thermal blanket and two ragged quilts I pilfered from the linen closet of the main house, and I wake each morning to frost-bitten air; my bones old and stiff. The kids' beds in the main house are piled high with blankets but I can't bring myself to ask them to give any of them up because I know they get just as cold as me and at least I have Shane's body heat under my covers.

Jillian's bed, in her hideaway attic bedroom, is so piled with blankets it resembles a cave. She took me up to her room once to try on clothes that don't fit her anymore. Jillian is 14 and I'm 25 but she's already a couple of sizes bigger than me. I had been curious what could be found in the bedroom of a fourteen year old girl growing up without a mother on a cattle ranch in Alaska. A quick glance around the room eases some of the maternal worries in me. It is a messy room with clothes and magazines strewn about and an old record player and several records on the floor in the corner. Yes, she has at least some of the things that girls need. There is a desk with books and papers on it facing a small round window where I imagine her sitting to do her homework or to write letters to friends and relatives in the lower 48. Several strings of colorful beads hang from the mirror on her dresser and a hairbrush full of lost strands of her silky blond hair, a tube of shiny lip-gloss and some eye shadow lay on top. Her mattress sits on a rough, unpainted wood platform built onto the floor. It brings to mind huge splinters that would call for a mom with a needle and a good pair of tweezers. I can't help but wonder if dads own tweezers.

Reluctantly each morning I pull myself up from my cocoon into a sitting position, my legs still beneath the covers, and layer on my two men's flannel shirts and the grey sweatshirt from Jillian. Then I swing out my legs and pull on a pair of pink tights with a runner along the left thigh. These tights have had a whole other life before finding their way to me. I imagine they danced on a stage, bathed in bright lights before being tossed into a huge black garbage bag with itchy sweaters and too-small sneakers for the Goodwill truck.

Between bites of crackers and pauses for deep breaths, willing the nausea to pass, I pull on my stiff, dirty jeans that can stand alone in the corner, and slip yesterday's socked feet into my trusty boots. My ponytail hangs down between my shoulder blades and I give it minimal attention. There's not much I can do with the thin, stringy mess. Shane gets dressed in much the same fashion but we don't speak. It's too cold, too dark. Words don't fit there.

These days are difficult from start to finish. Life has taken on a new color; gray. Dark gray. Weeks go by with no sunshine. They keep telling us that if we think this is hard, we will never survive the winter. They tell us that there is a man up the road who takes light therapy to get him through the darkest days of winter. I need light therapy already and I'm not even sure what it is. I want to go home. I need to go home. Shane wants to go too but won't admit it.

One day, out of the blue, Shane decides it's safe to make contact with someone back home. He gets permission to use the telephone and calls a buddy in Texas. They only talk for a minute or two. Shane gives him the address of the ranch and asks if he'd send us some cash, but not to tell anyone else he's heard from us. Dave says things are cool and that he'll send us what he can real soon. You can count on me, man. Dave is one of the many people Shane has given several sealed white envelopes to.

Every day after the call to Dave, one of us makes the long trek to the mailbox in anticipation of finding an envelope with our names on it. After ten days or so, just when I'm about to give up on Dave, I drive the 4-wheeler down the road to the mailbox, say a quick prayer, pull open the box, and there it is; one single small white envelope. I know what it is before I even see the writing. My heartbeat quickens and I look around to see if anyone is watching, like I've fallen down, embarrassed that someone might have seen. Quickly, before it vanishes into thin air, I reach for the envelope, glance at Shane's name on the front, stuff it into my pocket and put the 4-wheeler in gear. About a quarter mile down the road I stop and pull it out of my pocket, consider its weightiness and study the writing. No return address. Shane's name, c/o The Anchor Cattle Company, Homer, Alaska, has been scribbled in block letters with a black pen that is running out of ink. I feel like that pen, like I'm running out of ink, like soon I will be invisible if I stay here much longer; if I don't get home and prove to my family and friends that I still exist. I tear off a short end of the envelope and blow a puff of air into the opening. Inside there is another small white envelope folded down and sealed tight.

Later that night, in our bed with a warm fire burning in the stove, Shane opens the sealed envelope and spreads the money on top of the blankets. One thousand dollars! We are rich. Let's go home, I whisper, tears welling up in my eyes. For once, Shane doesn't tell me to be a strong soldier, to quit whining and be grateful for what we have. He just folds the money, puts it in the front pocket of his jeans and holds me tenderly like in the beginning. That night, the darkness is like an extra blanket, and I dream of home.

October 14, 1985
Today is daddy's birthday and I found myself thinking of him often. I hope he is happy and well. There are three more family birthdays to celebrate this month and if all goes well, I will be there with them when they roll around.

We took a hike up the mountain this afternoon. What a view - 180 degrees of snow-capped mountains and valleys and the bay down below. Saw some giant bear tracks on the road. Am reading on my 7th book since I've been here.

Have been feeling better last two days, except for some cramps. The hike today helped me gain back some of my strength. We've been keeping the mudroom full of cut split wood in anticipation of the first snow. I hope we see it before we leave.

October 18, 1985
Today was very cold. It snowed most of the day. This was our second snowfall; the first came on the 15th. The ground is barely covered with a soft blanket of white. It feels like Christmas.

Have been preparing to leave on the 20th. I confirmed our reservations with the airlines today. It will be a long, tiring journey, but I am looking forward to it. Haven't been sleeping well the past few nights.

Drove into town alone today. I made 3 or 4 stops, and then I ate at McDonalds. It felt like

such a treat! The roads were very slick. I stopped
at the bottom of the big hill, on the way home, and
put the truck in 4-wheel drive. It helped and I was
able to make it back without incident.

Wayne and some neighbors decide to send Shane and me back home in style with a huge crab boil the evening of our midnight flight from the Homer airport. We have even been allowed to take showers in anticipation of the long journey. The big guy who lives down the lane that we've only met two other times brings the crab. He's the one with the crab boat who is gone fishing most days. Mr. and Mrs. K. show up with pie, and the young couple from up the road, the ones who built their own cabin, is the last to arrive. Shane and I spent one or two nights at their place playing cards. She grows their vegetables and he grows their marijuana. They live a simple, private life in a very small and remote cabin with an indoor shower and sink, but an outdoor toilet. She loves my boots and we talk about the store in Anchorage where I found them. It reminds me of the day Mr. Tennessee drove off in our truck and the memory hangs over me like a dark cloud the rest of the evening.

There is prickly excitement in the air. Someone brought beer and all the men soon have a can in their rough-knuckled hands. It's a party! This may be the last get-together before winter sets in and weeks will go by without a glimpse of each other. There must be ten different conversations going and from under my cloud I let waves of happy noise, smiles and laughter crash against me. I know I will never see any of these wonderful people again after tonight. Shane is saying we'll be back after we take care of some business back home. Maybe those are his plans, but mine are different. I know I won't be back and suddenly tears are clumping into a tight ball in my throat. I am guilt-ridden. My circumstances have forced me to lie to these good people. Wayne, who welcomed us from the first day and never asked any questions; Mrs. K. who let me ignore her questions, made sure we had clothes to wear, encouraged me to buy the journal, shared her prized pie recipe with me, and insisted I swing in her yard like a carefree child. We were given an instant family and friends, a bed to sleep in, good food to eat, and the opportunity to earn it all through honest, hard work. I swallow hard past the lump, keeping the tears from rising.

Someone puts several layers of newspaper across the long table and everyone finds a seat. I have been relieved of kitchen duty and find that it feels nice to be served for a change when Wayne empties the first pot into the center of the table and it's a free-for-all as everyone grabs what they want from huge steaming piles of fresh crab. There are no utensils, no pliers or tiny forks for digging the last string of sweet, white meat from the corners. You just use the tools God gave you, Wayne says, breaking off a leg, bending it in half until it snaps, and sucking the huge delicate morsel into his mouth with a satisfied smile.

After everyone has had more than enough to eat, it is time to gather our bags for the quick drive to the airport. There are hugs and promises in our good-byes, and as Shane and I pile into the cab of the truck with Wayne, it begins to snow. As Wayne pulls out of the yard, I turn to face the back window and wave a final good-bye. Now I cannot swallow the tears away. Shane stares straight ahead, his eyes trained on the high beams lighting our way. He is changing before my very eyes. In the shadowy light I can see his jaw muscles tighten and loosen, tighten and loosen; his mind already in Texas where nothing good waits for him.

When we arrive at the Homer airport, the snow is coming down thick and chunky and the wind blows it straight into our faces. Wayne hurries to get the door. I'm behind Shane; the green army duffel bag containing both our clothes hanging from his left shoulder. I am so focused on this journey that it doesn't occur to me that this snowstorm might cause our flight to be canceled. But inside the terminal, several passengers are standing around, cups of steaming coffee warming their hands, speculating whether or not any of us would be going anywhere any time soon. As I brush snow off my arms and shake it out of my hair, I catch the words de-icing, cancelation, and postponement being thrown around the room. My heart sinks. I am holding my breath again as we step up to the counter and show the attendant our tickets; the tickets bearing alias names; the $199.00 super saver tickets that, in two days' time, will take us from Homer to Anchorage, Anchorage to Seattle, Seattle to Salt Lake City, Salt Lake City to Omaha, Omaha to Houston and finally, Houston to Dallas/Fort Worth.

Chapter Eighteen

Shane and I are both in jail. It is early March 1986. I am 6 months pregnant and have been locked up in the Wise County jail for five days with no idea what is going on beyond these cell walls. Tonight they have brought Shane in and put him in the cell next to mine. I cannot see him, but I can hear his hysterical screaming through the air vent. I don't know if he knows I'm on the other side of the wall and I don't know if I want him to. We haven't spoken or seen each other since Christmas and suddenly, just like with a spring thunderstorm, he is here all thunder and lightning and wreaking all kinds of havoc.

The weight of my world is so unbearable that my old bag of tricks is obsolete. I try to count and spell to keep my mind busy but the loops don't take hold, the words I'm spelling just drop out of my brain abandoning me. I am a basket case barely holding it together.

Shane has been yelling at the top of his lungs on and off for hours. I learn that he has already spent a couple of weeks in the Palo Pinto County jail before being extricated here to Wise County. I learn that he too is in a cell by himself and he keeps asking for a Mr. Cruz. I've never heard this name before and I wonder if it's his attorney. There is so much angst, anger and emotion in his screaming that it draws me closer to the air vent connecting our cells. Even now, with a cinderblock wall between us he has a strong, magnetic pull on me. I sit on the floor in the dark, the side of my head glued to the vent, his words stinging my ears and tugging at my heart.

The next day he is still yelling. I feel compelled to start writing down the things he is saying because I don't know what else to do. I think maybe his attorney might want to know this stuff. I think what if he's telling the truth and I just sit here and do nothing. I think that it just might be the psychotic rantings of a demented, tortured soul and that my husband has completely lost his mind, but what if he hasn't? Even now I am honor-bound to help him if I can.

After a while, listening and writing wears me out and I realize that I cannot bear the weight of his world and mine too and there is nothing else to do but succumb to the collective pressure of our collided worlds and sob until sleep takes over. I wake to my baby kicking and moving inside me, and my husband screaming still:

<u>March 1, 1986 late night and March 2, 1986 early a.m. and all day</u>.

"They're killing me. They're going to shoot me.

[The Sheriff] has already killed once and I'm going to be next.

[The Sheriff] "is setting me up with false charges because I know too much.

If I get quiet ya'll will know what happened.

Watch what you say and do because everything is recorded.

Mr. Cruz I need your help.

I'm in here without clothes or a mattress.

[Sheriff], you know I didn't do it, so why are you doing this to me?

Get my wife out of this situation right now – she doesn't belong in here."

Oh God! He knows I'm here. My heart begins to pound. I panic. I can barely breathe. I begin to pace the six-foot cell. Back and forth, back and forth, back and forth. I felt safer when I thought he didn't know I was here. Just the thought of having to deal with him wears me out. I don't want any trouble. I just want to get out of here. The Sheriff hasn't given me a chance to tell my side of the story. I don't want to do or say anything now that might jeopardize my freedom. I am not guilty of the charges they have brought against me. I am waiting for my day in court. I am waiting for a visit from my attorney. I am waiting for a chance to get on with my life. I crouch in the corner, sink to the floor and try to make myself invisible.

After a while the night jailer comes to Shane's cell door and I hear the jailer tell him that if he doesn't stop yelling he'll bring three deputies in to shut him up.

The jailer's threats do not work. Shane continues to yell:

"You're just mad because you didn't find a lab".

Then he says someone is in his cell with him – that they know his name but he doesn't know theirs. He bursts out responses as if someone is talking to him.

"You're going to shoot me right out front?

I see you looking at me.

SOMEONE GET IN HERE FAST"!!!

This outburst brings me to my feet and I pace some more, my heart pounding again. Then it's quiet. I don't hear anything. I think maybe they have taken him somewhere else. It's quiet for a long time. I curl up on the hard mattress. There is no pillow, but I draw the itchy army blanket up to my neck and close my eyes.

He starts yelling again:

"It's going to be alright now baby".
Then:
"Get in here and get me Cruz before these mother fuckers kill me.

Get this damn door open and get these mother fuckers away from me.

No, you son-of-a-bitch don't pull that trigger, you better hold on.

I see you shining a light on me.

I'm back here Mr. Cruz! Get me out of here and don't let them have a gun on.

If you guys move me you're going to be fucked up.

HELP! HELP! HELP"!
I hear the Jailer walk up to Shane's door again. He brings someone with him. They say, "Come and talk to us."
Shane says "No way". His voice is starting to crack.
Someone says, "I'll protect you."
He doesn't go with them.
"You're the murderer, get it right.

You burned your ass that night you tried to burn mine.

Help, Help, HELP!

You better get the fuck out of here with that gun.

Don't mess with my rights, I'm an American".

The jailer returns with someone else. They ask Shane to come out and talk to them. He says no, that he's afraid for his life. They ask why he is afraid of them. He says; "You know why I'm afraid of you". Shane asks for them to bring his attorney and then he'll go with them. They leave without taking Shane with them.

<u>March 3, 1986 early a.m.</u>
"I want to see my lawyer".

The Jailer comes back and says; "Haven't you got all that out of your system"?

Shane says, "I don't know what you're talking about".

The Jailer says, "You should".

Shane: "Hey everyone, can you hear me? I'm still alive".

He asks to see his lawyer all day.

He keeps saying he is being framed, that he did not kill anyone.

He says the Sheriff killed [that guy].

He's asking for a shower. His voice is sounding very strained.

"I didn't tell you that, his brother-in-law did, remember?

Don't you know I can hear everything y'all say up there?

I heard you, you said red hair, he has red hair and he's not in jail.

Someone come and get me. They're covering up a murder and pinning it on me.

I was trying to help you.

You're just trying to railroad me and Vanessa.

I want my lawyer.

I'll tell him the side of the story you don't know.

You killed [that guy].

He said the suspect had red hair.

I heard him on the phone.

[The Sheriff] killed [that guy].

Someone investigate this – please!

His sister's husband.

Brother-in-law – not brother.

I didn't kill anyone. I have proof. I can prove where I was that whole week."

<u>March 4, 1986</u>
It is quiet all day. He asks to see his lawyer, that's all. His voice is all but gone.

Around midnight he starts asking for his lawyer again and starts screaming for help…saying they were going to kill him NOW!

During the hours when Shane is not screaming, I pass the time by reading, sleeping and doing a little exercise. The cell I'm in is a block with two separate cells with metal bar doors and a little hallway that the cell doors open on to. The other cell is empty for most of the days I'm there, except for one weekend when they bring in four or five girls and most are sleeping on the floor anywhere they can find a spot. They all seem to know who I am and what I'm in for. They give me my space and I get to keep my cell all to myself.

My cell door and the other cell door are always left open so I can pace the length of my cell which is about 8 feet, out into the hall, which is about four feet by eight feet, then to the far wall in the next cell and back again. I must make this trip fifty times a day for the twelve days I'm here. I also do several intervals of 25 jumping jacks and 10 push-ups every day, as best I can with my bulging belly.

Each cell has a sink, a toilet and a shower. There is no hot water and cold showers are a bitch but I force myself to take one every other day. My family brings me some writing paper, pencils and paperback books. I also get to have toothpaste, a toothbrush, soap and a few changes of clothes.

I pray a lot and sleep a lot and try not to think the worst. I daydream a great deal and picture myself holding my baby girl, for now I know, even without proof, that I am carrying the baby girl Shane said he gave me when we were in Alaska so many months ago. I try to imagine what her little face will look like, and how warm and perfect she will feel in my arms.

<u>March 5, 1986</u>
It is quiet all day until the evening.

"Sheriff, now I know you shot that cop.

He must have had something on you.

You killed that detective.

Someone in Dallas is working with [the Sheriff] to pin it on me."

The jailer comes back to talk to Shane.
"I haven't had any soap in four days and would like a wash cloth and fresh towel to take a shower.

I'd also like to see my lawyer."

The jailer asks if he had the number. The jailer says he'll get back to him.

"Vanessa, I never killed no cop or anyone else.

You better get out of here with that gun.

Vanessa, I know too much now.

I figured it out and now he's going to have to kill me, so you have [the Sheriff] investigated.

Help! Help! Help!

Come get me.

I know what's happening.

Vanessa, I heard him say they're going to kill you too."

Vanessa May, 1986

Chapter Nineteen

Shane and I go our separate ways shortly after our marathon Super Shuttle flight lands at the Dallas Fort Worth International Airport on October 21, 1985.

October 24, 1985
Been back on familiar ground three days now. I haven't talked to or seen any family. Will probably get to Austin this weekend. Tomorrow is Tiffany's birthday – would like to be there, we'll see. The heat is taking its toll on our bodies, which have grown used to a cooler climate. The trip did prove tiring, but we survived. After all, we are survivors! Our friends have been very gracious in putting us up these past few days. I know it hasn't been easy for them.

My Mom and sister Mary are very happy and surprised to find me on their doorstep in Austin that weekend. I have arrived alone and unannounced after being gone for more than three months. After retrieving our Corvette from a friend's garage, I leave Shane in Fort Worth so he can "take care of business" and I head south. There are hugs and tears and questions and more hugs on the Austin front porch before we finally make our way inside. Over the next few days I tell them some of what I've been through. I tell them how beautiful Alaska is. I tell them about Moses and Wayne and Curtis and Jill and all about the cattle ranch. I tell them about the huge strawberries and the rhubarb pie I got so good at making, and I tell them about Stubby the calf I fed with a bottle. They can't believe I have been working as a cook for room and board. I tell them about the hitchhiker and losing all our money and I tell them I think I'm pregnant.

Teresa, my big sister, is in the waiting room of the doctor's office. I'm wearing a hospital gown open in the back and am sitting cross-legged on the examining table. I've already left my urine specimen in the tiny bathroom and heard the nurse retrieve it through the little door in the wall a few minutes ago. The doctor walks in looking at my chart and introduces himself. This is my sister's doctor. He delivered my nephew, Christopher and is going to deliver the baby she's carrying now, which is due in January.

You're going to have a baby.

He doesn't waste any time. He just ups and tells me I'm going to have a baby. He doesn't tell me that I'm pregnant; he tells me that I'm going to have a baby and the weight and magnitude of these words set my soul free. It is real. It is confirmed. It is 100% true and I am speechless and my heart does somersaults while my mind grabs on to the thought of this baby with a fierceness that I didn't know was in me. There is another human being growing inside me and now, instantly, the world is different.

November 10, 1985
I found out on October 31st that I'm expecting a baby!!! It seems so unreal. I'm still not sure I believe it's finally happened to me! According to

the doctor's calculations, it will be due in mid-May. I am thrilled, scared and relieved. I've wanted a baby for so long and now when my life is upside down, I manage to become pregnant. I have decided not to drift back into my former lifestyle. Now that I am finally back home again, I don't want to do anything to mess it up. The most difficult aspect of that decision will be explaining it to Shane. We have been apart for almost two weeks now and have not been in contact. I know he will not like what I have to say but I must stand firm with my decision and make him realize it is the only reasonable thing for me to do. I don't like the idea of keeping his baby from him but I dislike even more the thought of raising our child in an unhealthy, unsure world of drug users and immorality. I know I'm not perfect but I want only good things for myself and my baby from now on. I'm positive it's the right thing to do.

Shane bounces in and out of my life over the next couple of months. When he comes to visit I pack a little bag and the two of us check into a nearby motel and spend two or three days in bed together. I'm still not really showing and I'm not in maternity clothes yet. Sometimes I think Shane forgets that I'm pregnant. Every once in a while, after we have shared a tender moment and we're lying in bed together, I work up the courage to talk to him about the dreams I have for our baby. I try to paint a picture for him, a picture without fear and junkies and drug dealing and dirty money. The picture of a life we can both be proud of; where love and health and vitality and nurturing bathe this precious child in comfort and security. Once or twice I can see his eyes trying to focus on the picture and sometimes the corners of his mouth start to turn up when he catches a glimpse of it, but in a fit of anger, he jumps out of the bed, and begins pacing around the room threatening my life if I ever try to take his child away from him. So I calm him with gentle promises while I pray with a sad heart for him to leave town again soon. I don't want anything bad to happen to him, but I know in my soul's core that it will take a miracle for my hopes and dreams to ever come true.

It is almost a month after my mom and I watch in horror as the Space Shuttle Challenger explodes into a million pieces on live TV. I will never forget that twisting, smoky image we all viewed over and over again, heartbroken for the families of the seven crew members lost forever. It is burned into my brain, just like the look on my baby sister, Jeanie's face when she is forced to leave me in the office of the FBI at the Federal Building in downtown Fort Worth.

There is a warrant for my arrest. The charge is possession of a controlled substance. They have convinced me that it is in my own best interest to turn myself. It will look better on my record than if they have to come get me.

I'm six months pregnant and scared to death but with a surprisingly calm exterior. Daddy got a phone call from the FBI. They say they know

I'm in Austin and that the sooner I come in, the better. They give me the impression that if I come in, we'll talk, they'll go easy on me and then I can go home. But that's not what happens. Jeanie is forced to leave me there and I can see the shock and fear in her eyes and there is nothing I can do to console her. We barely get a chance to say goodbye. I know it is killing her leaving me there, but it all happens so fast. I take out my diamond earrings and give them to her, we steal a quick hug and they lead her away.

After she's gone, they handcuff me and drive me over to the Tarrant County jail and lock me up. No questions, no talking, no chance to tell my side of the story. It's so unfair. They don't even look at me. I'm treated like a criminal, like I'm beneath them, and they have no time or inclination to speak to me. They don't tell me anything – there's no communication and that's the worst part. That's what breaks you down – the not knowing. At the jail, I get finger printed, photographed, stripped, searched, disinfected and put in a cellblock, my belly pulling tight against the orange jumpsuit I'm given as a replacement for the clothes I was wearing when I arrived at the Federal Building. Other female criminals sit around a small television at a round picnic table as I'm escorted to my cell. I'm carrying a thin mattress and a wool blanket and am silently shown to a cell. Thankfully I am mostly ignored by the other women in the pod. I place the mattress on the bed frame and lay down, covering myself with the blanket. It's noisy and cold and very bright. At some point, everyone is instructed to go to their cells, the cell doors are electronically closed and the lights go out.

The next day I'm transported to the Wise County jail. I still don't know what's going on. No one will talk to me.

Chapter Twenty

May 4, 1986

Hello. A lot has happened the past few months. I hardly know where to begin. The authorities arrested Shane early in February. He is still in jail. The FBI called daddy and told him to talk me into surrendering, so I did – on February 23, 1986. I spent 12 days in jail and was finally released on a PR bond by the Sheriff. We are both waiting to stand trial and meanwhile, our baby is due in 11 days.

I am living with daddy because it was a stipulation of the court at a bond reduction hearing. My bond was originally set at $50,000. It was lowered to $10,000 after 10 days in jail and then they let me out.

Shane's charged with two things and his bond is $100,000.

We each have our lawyers – his is court appointed and I'm struggling to pay for mine. We have both been through too much and will be glad when it's all over. Our futures are both so uncertain and I cannot begin to make any decisions yet about a possible reconciliation. We will have to wait it out and make the best of the court's decisions.

Still, we are excited about the baby. It will be very difficult to adjust, but I've waited so long for it to happen. I'm sure everything is fine and the delivery will be normal and event-free.

I pray for all of us every day.

The judge says I must stay in the area so I move in with Daddy and my stepmother, Donna. Daddy worries about me being pregnant and home alone all day so he arranges for my sister, Mary, to move up from Austin to be with me. She and I are sharing a queen size bed in one room and Tiffany, her three-year old daughter, is sharing a room with Donna's youngest daughter, "little Mary" who is in the 6th grade.

My only job is to get little Mary up and ready for school each morning. She can be a hateful little girl and acts out often. She does not like being woken up. One morning when I'm about 8 months pregnant, she kicks me in the stomach as hard as she can when I try to wake her up. I'm so stunned, hurt and frightened that my first response is to slap her hard across the face. She runs to the phone and calls Donna at work to tell her mom that I have hit her for no reason. Donna believes little Mary, and a rift is born between us that never heals.

It is a difficult living situation on so many levels that Mary and I begin planning to move as soon as my Natalie Dawn is born. This is the name I have settled on after months of thinking, reading, searching through baby name books and fretting over the perfect name.

My labor begins around 3:00 am. This child is almost two weeks late and I feel like I am about to explode. For three hours, I lie awake in bed next to Mary, who is sleeping soundly, and I time the pains which remain consistently about 10 minutes apart. At 6:00 am when I hear Daddy's alarm ring, I wake up Mary and ask her to tell Daddy that I think it's time.

Daddy has to go to work earlier than Donna, so Donna drives me to John Peter Smith Hospital where I get checked in, and then she leaves for work. The nurses, who are none too friendly, hook an IV to my arm, give me an enema and leave me in a room the size of a small closet – with an attached two-piece bathroom - there is barely room for the bed. I am all alone with my contractions that never subside...they remain ten minutes apart for an eternity. There is no one to talk to and no TV. Connie and her mom, Joan, come by around 11:00 am and keep me company for a while. It is so nice to have someone there with me to help pass the time but eventually they must leave. Later, when the IV has been dry for hours, the hospital must go through a shift change because a new nurse walks in obviously startled to find me there. She unhooks the IV and sends in a doctor to check me. It is mid-afternoon and I have only dilated to 3cm. They leave me again and I don't see anyone else until Connie comes back in the late afternoon. I'm really glad she's here with me because no one else could make it. We talk and laugh and listen to women in nearby rooms making their way through their own labors. At one point a very loud succession of "Mamma Mias" coming from a nearby room makes us snicker, and then grow quiet, our minds lost inside our own fears. Soon I want to scream my own Mamma Mia as my contractions morph into a near unbearable constant, pulsing pain (pain seems too kind and gentle a word for what I'm experiencing) for surely I am being turned inside out. I am growing delirious from no rest, no food, no water and no drugs.

I've been coming to John Peter Smith (JPS), the local county hospital for my regular check-ups ever since I got out of jail. Being six months pregnant and in jail is not something I would ever recommend to anyone, and in hindsight I probably should have let the FBI come after me if they wanted me so badly. It has been a roller-coaster ride, that's for sure. JPS gives about 100 women (I use this term loosely because most of them are very young teen-agers) appointments all for 8:00 am. It is first-come, first-served so I learn quickly to arrive early, and by early I mean 6:30 am, so I'm one of the first few in line when they open the doors at eight. If you don't get there until 8:00 you better be ready to wait all day to be seen. I never see the same doctor twice and don't know who will deliver my baby. They make us sit through some classes to learn how to change diapers and make bottles and I appreciate the effort, but I really think I can do this without their help. They also give us birth control pills to start taking immediately after giving birth because they don't want to see us back in here any time soon. At these appointments I'm always the oldest pregnant woman there and most of the others barely speak English. I have little in common with these women other than the fact that we are all growing another human being inside our bodies.

The one class I wish I had paid better attention to is the one that taught us how to breathe through the pains, because I am out of control as the day turns into night. At some point a doctor decides I have progressed sufficiently to be moved to the "Active Labor" room. No one is allowed inside this place where women wait on gurneys along the walls of a long room, so Connie goes home and I don't think I have a chance to thank her for being there with me all these hours.

I am so out of my mind with pain and from dehydration that I'm pretty sure I fall in and out of consciousness. There have been and will be no drugs for me through this process. I have no money and therefore get the bare-bones treatment. I really feel like a nobody when after a particularly painful contraction which brings a series of blood-curdling screams from my lips, a hateful nurse comes over to me, brings her angry face within inches of mine, sticks her index finger up to my nose and vehemently tells me to shut up!

Around 2:00 am, after about 22 hours of labor, someone discovers that my water still has not broken, so an instrument resembling a very long crochet hook is used and viola! my contractions triple in intensity and there is no more holding back the screams. Not long after having my water broken, I am wheeled into the operating room and introduced to the doctor who will be bringing my baby into this world. This is the first time I've seen this particular doctor and she seems nice enough and frankly I don't care as long as she can get me through to the other side of this excruciatingly brutal experience. There is a flurry of activity and someone is telling me to push. I am so disoriented and unsure of anything that I don't know if I am pushing or not, but in my mind I am telling every muscle in my body to push. It must be working because within minutes, they are laying a pink baby in my arms and it is my beautiful baby girl who I love instantly and purely and ferociously.

It is 3:45 in the morning, the day after I went into labor, and suddenly I am a mother. I have given birth to a beautiful baby girl! And as I'm looking into her eyes that seem to be looking through to my soul, I start to panic because this baby does not look like a Natalie Dawn. I want desperately to say something to her, to welcome her to the world, and tell her how much I love her and that I will always be here for her but I can't speak because my mouth is so dry that my tongue is stuck. It is an inch thick and glued to the roof of my mouth and I can only look at my sweet angel baby through my tears of overwhelming joy. Within seconds, they take her from me and I fall into a deep sleep.

It isn't long before I'm waking up in the recovery room dying of thirst. A nurse brings me some orange juice and waits while I drink it down. Soon I am choking on something that feels stuck in my throat. I cough and feel something land on my tongue. Then I swallow and it's in my throat again. The nurse helps me to the ladies room and while I'm in there, I cough and look in the mirror to see if I can get rid of this thing that is choking me. And there it is, there is something slimy and tissue-like on my tongue so I grab it, but it slips out of my fingers and snaps to the back of my throat. I look again and realize it is my uvula. But it is severely stretched out of shape and translucent. I estimate that it is about three inches long and as big around as my thumb. When I get back to my bed, I call the nurse over and open my mouth so she too can see this unbelievable thing. She must see lots of unusual things in her line of work, but it is clear she has never seen anything like this before. She is freaked and runs out of the room with a gasp. She quickly returns with a couple of doctors and nurses and they all take turns looking inside my mouth. It's obvious none of them have ever seen a uvula in such a state and they don't know what to do about it. So they do nothing, and luckily by the next day my uvula is almost back to normal. It is never mentioned again. But to this day, I snore like a drunken sailor and when I catch a cold my uvula will swell and hang down my throat for a day or so until it shrinks back again.

Later that morning I get visitors while I'm holding my Sweet Angel Baby Tiger Lily in my arms. This is the pet name that springs from my heart when I am holding her for the first time since giving birth. I have her in my lap and I have unwrapped the blankets and am marveling at her tiny fingers and toes, the unbelievable softness of her skin and the smell of her - which is so much like the smell of her daddy it throws me for a loop. I know I must choose a different name for her but nothing but Sweet Angel Baby Tiger Lily has come to mind.

Mary is here and so are Connie and her mom. Joan can't get over how long my baby's fingers and toes are...a definite trait from my side of the family! And her fingernails are so long they wrap around the ends of her fingers. I silently worry how I'm going to trim them without hurting her.

As I'm caressing my sweet cooing baby, a name that I haven't thought of in years springs into my mind. I had met a woman in Cleburne named Shalyn in 1981 when I worked at City Hall and I really liked the name, storing it in the back of my mind in case I ever had a baby girl. I don't know why I haven't thought of it the whole time I've been pregnant, but here it is, suddenly at the forefront of my mind and I know it is right for this sweet child of mine. Shalyn has just named herself and she is perfect, and all is right with the world, except that her daddy is in jail waiting trial for attempted capital murder, her mommy has charges pending against her as well, we have no money, owe an attorney thousands of dollars and we have nothing to our names. But right now, in this moment I can let all that go and I honestly see a bright future for both of us, somewhere down the road.

Vanessa and Shalyn, 1987

Chapter Twenty-One

Shalyn is three months old. I cannot get enough of her. She is beautiful, happy, funny, good-natured and I love her more than I could ever have imagined. She sleeps in a crib two feet from my side of the queen bed Mary and I share. We are together day and night and I wouldn't have it any other way. She has brought the kind of joy into my life that I've always craved. I love taking care of her. We have our routines and the simplicity of our days have grounded me in the best way. I hold her in my arms and still cannot believe she is mine. I feed her, bathe her, read her stories and sing her lullabies and my life is complete. But we are cramped, we are imposing on Daddy and Donna, and we want to get a place of our own but it's just not possible right now. Mary and I talk late into the nights envisioning a home of our own where we can raise our daughters and carve out a life for ourselves. I desperately need to start thinking of getting a job but the thought of leaving Shalyn breaks my heart.

Motherhood has not changed me; it has made me who I am. We eat and sleep and breathe as humans, but as mothers we break and bleed and fast and don't sleep so our baby can eat and thrive and grow, and through our sacrifices we are stronger and happier and fuller and richer and better humans than we were before. No one could have told me these things would happen to me - that my being would be so transformed, that my world would be bigger and my focus so intense.

Shane will be going to prison soon to serve two concurrent, ten-year sentences. This news brings me tremendous relief and great sadness - suffocating guilt and soaring freedom. He has opted for a plea bargain rather than going to trial. I'm not clear on the details and a plea bargain doesn't sound like his style, but I'm not inclined to inquire, as I still have my own legal problems to figure out. I've read and re-read the journal I kept of his haunting, desperate screams while I was in the jail cell next to him. I've had a lot of time to think about him, about us and about this beautiful baby girl we made and I always come back to what feels true in my heart. The truth is that there is no place for Shane here.

I think he is mentally ill and that he has been self-medicating with Valium, marijuana and a myriad of other sedatives the whole time I've known him. He's been writing me letters full of fantastical outbursts of paranoia and suspicions. He thinks the government has implanted a device inside his brain and can read his thoughts through radio waves. He thinks he holds top-secret information that the enemy is trying to extract from his mind. He goes on and on about God and religion and the end of the world. Connie is a social worker with the local mental health and mental retardation facility and tells me these are common symptoms of paranoid schizophrenia and the sting of her words ring true. Patients often focus on sex, politics or religion. Shane shows signs of focusing on all three in his terrifying letters. It frightens me every time I open the mailbox and find another envelope with my name and address in his penciled hand. I want to distance myself from him. I don't want him to write me anymore and I don't want to write back. I certainly don't want to see him. But I need to go visit him in Wise County before they transfer him to Huntsville. I need him to sign a power of attorney that will put $11,000 into my hands.

I find out that Shane has a bank account in Grand Prairie that's in his name only. The balance is just under $11,000. I've been in touch with the bank and they will only release the money to me if I have Shane's signature on a power of attorney. I know Shane will only sign it if he thinks I will use the money to hire an attorney to try to overturn his convictions. I also know that I owe my attorney $5,000, my charges are still pending and I don't know what is going to happen to me. I could still end up in prison myself. I've got to take action, make something happen for myself. Shane taught me that much. Besides, Texas is a community property state; I know that half of that money is mine, and I'm making the executive decision to use his half on our daughter. Within days, my attorney sends me the power of attorney that just may change everything, at least for Shalyn and me. I dress my sweet angel baby in a bright, sunny outfit and tell her we are going to go see her daddy.

It is the only time Shane and Shalyn are ever in each other's presence. It is a painful, bittersweet visit. She screams the whole time he is holding her. And it's no wonder because we are in a bright institutional visitor's room, there are guards all around us, Shane is shackled at his ankles and sitting on a metal bench. I thought he would hold her more naturally, but he doesn't seem to know what to do. He doesn't cuddle her, kiss her or speak softly into her ears. He holds her extended from his body like a trophy and she does not like it.

She is working herself into a fit. I have never seen her like this and it breaks my heart. I take her from him, hold her tight against me the way she likes, and rock her gently. Within seconds she is no longer crying. I take this moment to pull the power of attorney from my purse and hand it to Shane. Someone gives him a pen and he is signing. We have discussed it beforehand and he knows that he's signing a piece of paper to let me get the money out of the bank account in Grand Prairie. He knows how much money it is and he says to me that this is going to change everything. That he feels like this is the big break we've needed for a long time. I feel I might burst any moment if I don't get out of there quick. The entire visit takes less than 15 minutes.

Chapter Twenty-Two

It is August 1986 when Mary, Tiffany, me, and Shalyn move into the "red" house in Southwest Fort Worth. It is a four bedroom, two bath brick house (trimmed in brick red paint) with a two-car garage and a large backyard. The rent is $575 per month, utilities are about $100 and we get by on less than $40 per week on groceries. I have paid my attorney bill in full, the charges against me have been dropped and I start a new job on Monday. Shane was right about one thing; this money has changed everything. Deep in my heart, on some level, I believe Shane will forgive me for doing what I had to do.

I give Daddy a thousand dollars for letting me and Shalyn live with him, and for bringing Mary up from Austin to be with me. It has really been wonderful having her here. We have grown much closer and have found that we live together well. I can't imagine getting through these last few months without her love, support and easy laughter. After paying first and last months' rent, buying some work clothes and setting up our household, I still have a little nest egg in the bank for a rainy day, but right now the sun is definitely shining on our little world.

Having the 'possession' charge against me dismissed right around the time Mary and I move is kind of a non-event. After all the angst and worry over the past few months, it seems too easy for my attorney to just call me one day and say it's done – it is all over, they've decided to drop the charges – you'll get a copy of the Order of Dismissal in the mail. What? Are you sure? He assures me this is, in fact, the case and thanks me for my business. I hang up the phone and scream in relief. There is no official celebration but the weight of my world is suddenly lighter and my smiles come easier now.

I am working in the purchasing department at Stearns Airport Equipment during the day making $6.00 an hour while Mary stays home with the girls. When I get home from work, we enjoy a quick family dinner around the kitchen table and Mary heads off to Tarrant County Junior College where she is working on finishing her associate's degree. On the weekends, Mary waits tables for some spending money of her own. Our budget is so tight there is barely $5 left after paying the bills but we are thriving in so many ways. For months I do not leave the house for anything except work but I am very happy. My evenings are full and rich with dishes, laundry, playing with the kids, bath time, reading stories and sleep. Tiffany and Shalyn are healthy, happy and growing like weeds.

Sometimes I sit and watch Shalyn sleeping and I swear I can see her grow. It's like she inhales, and "pouf" she is suddenly ever so slightly bigger than she was. I love looking at her sweet face. Those full pink lips, the cute slightly turned up nose, the perfectly arched eyebrows, and those puffy chipmunk cheeks are so big you just want to smother them in kisses. And when I do, she giggles from her belly and squeals with joy. She is a happy, content, bright baby with so much personality.

She and I share the master bedroom. Her crib is at the foot of my bed and she has trained me well to get up two or three times a night to give her a drink of juice. I read and sing songs to her every night and cherish our quiet little sanctuary. Early on Saturday mornings I take her out of her crib and bring her back to bed with me. We talk and laugh and doze and enjoy each other's company. It is the only lazy part of our week.

Shalyn has talked since the day she was born. It's like she is telling full and rich stories with her limited ability to make sounds. Her tone rises and falls, she uses inflection and places emphasis on certain parts, her face is completely animated and I listen intently and respond in kind. I talk to her all the time and I can see in her eyes that she is listening and comprehending on many levels. Her eyes focus on my mouth when I'm spelling words to her. I tell her that the sky is blue and the grass is green, g-r-e-e-n. I tell her that God's glory is all around us and it is up to us to see it every day. I explain about the magic of flowers and sunsets and rainbows to her cooing and her happy baby gurgles. She loves picture books and I spend hours making up stories about the puppies and kittens and kites on the pages and she is delighted. She is my Sweet Angel Baby Tiger Lily and I am overwhelmed sometimes at how blessed we are. It is easy when I look at her perfect sweet face, with those big green eyes, to know she is going to grow into a beautiful woman. I know she will be strong-willed, self-assured and elegant. She is intelligent and brave and kind and loving. I know these things. She is fearless and happy and loves deeply. I can tell even now, when she is only a few months old, that she is so very special and just may change the world.

She has so much of me in her, but she is definitely Shane's daughter too. She smells just like him. I know it's an odd thing to say, but they sweat the same sweat. And when she gets mad, her left eye squinches just like his. And when she gets angry or cries, her face and chest get all red and splotchy like him. I think she looks more like him but everyone tells me she looks just like me and that makes me happy.

It is a good thing that raising a child takes 18 years because right now I cannot imagine her going off to school, or learning to drive, or dating boys. God prepares us for those things gently over time. I would be happy if she never grows up and just stays this sweet perfect four-month old baby forever. I especially don't want to think of her driving and possibly having a horrifying accident like I did.

I'm 17 years old, exactly a year before I meet Shane at Spencer's Corner. It is a Sunday and I have just worked a double shift as a waitress at the Village Inn Pancake House – a favorite breakfast spot for the enlisted men and women stationed at Carswell Air Force Base, which is right down the street. I work every day after school from 3-10 and then I work Saturday and Sunday mornings as well. The tips aren't great (I'm happy if I get a dollar per table) but on a good weekend I come home with over $100 in my pocket. I'm earning 90 cents an hour plus tips and I always have money. Before I move in with Connie, I keep most of it in a big bowl on my dresser. Jeanie admits to me years later that she takes a handful every morning for lunch money and candy after school. Now that I've moved, I make regular deposits to my savings account at a little savings and loan on Highway 80.

It's about 6:30 pm and I'm driving home (to Connie's house). It's just a few days before we start our senior year at Western Hills High School. I'm living with Connie's family because my dad has moved to the Mid-Cities and I don't want to change high schools again. I would like to graduate with my friends. I do eventually end up moving to the mid-cities and living with Daddy again, but for a few months, I'm with Connie's family. Her parents are gracious enough to let me stay with them and I am sharing a room with Connie and her younger sister, Sandy.

I'm driving my dad's 1964 Volkswagen convertible bug because my Vega and its aluminum-sleeved engine are in the shop again. The year is 1977. We are not yet required by law to fasten our seatbelts and this car does not have any anyway. The glass is also not the safety kind. The driver of the car in front of me on Highway 377 stops to turn left but I don't see him because I have dozed off behind the wheel. I slam into that car and my face breaks a hole in the windshield while my knees slam into the metal dash and my chest hits the steering wheel. The first thing I realize is that my legs hurt like heck so I look down at them and a river of blood is gushing from my face. A nice lady helps me from the car and sits on the ground with my head in her lap. I know I am getting blood all over her but she acts like it's no big deal and tells me not to worry about anything as she strokes my hair gently, asking me questions in a very calm voice. Someone calls an ambulance. The guy I hit and his girlfriend are hovering over us intently. A doctor passing by stops and instructs someone to put ice on my face and someone does it. Some middle school kids on their bikes gather nearby trying to get a glimpse. A telephone repairman on a nearby pole sees the whole thing happen and ends up buying the totaled VW from my dad a few days later. He had been admiring the car coming down the road and saw the whole accident happen.

At the hospital I'm waiting for my dad to arrive because I'm a minor and they won't touch me until he gets there. Daddy walks in about the same time as the plastic surgeon; who, upon arrival, takes one quick look at my face and asks if anyone found any of the missing pieces. This is my first indication as to how bad things really are and I try not to panic at the thought of pieces of my face being gone. Donna is there and she goes back to the scene of the wreck with a jar of formaldehyde and actually brings back pieces of my face that are found stuck to the windshield.

The surgery takes about five hours and they successfully sew my nose back together, which has been split open two ways. The space between my upper lip and nose is mangled and they use some of the recovered tissue and some skin from my thigh to stitch up that area, and my forehead is split open from hairline to eyebrow. All the while, several nurses pick pieces of glass out of my arms and legs and talk with me to keep me calm. I have to remain awake during the surgery so I don't go into a coma from anesthesia. They give me several local anesthetic shots that hurt so bad it feels like they're injecting me with fire. After all is said and done, they say I have about 250 stitches in my face, but soon I'll be good as new, so I believe them. The surgeon says that it is a good thing someone thought to put ice on my face because otherwise, I would have been too swollen to operate on and the scarring would have been much worse.

I'm in the hospital for four days. Connie visits and sneaks in some fast food. My sisters come with Daddy and Donna and are warned not to stare or mention stitches or scars. The hospital staff has also removed the mirror from my room. My boyfriend, Mitch, comes by and so does the guy I hit. Everyone is upbeat and happy that I'm alive and so am I, and I heal quickly.

The guy whose car I hit is very sweet and concerned for me but I am worried about his car. Turns out Daddy isn't carrying insurance on the bug, as he has just recently finished restoring it and hadn't planned on anyone driving it until my car went into the shop unexpectedly, so I have to pay for the damage I've done to this guy's Oldsmobile. It comes to just under $1,000 and that's how much I have in my savings account, so all is well.

I start my senior year with some pretty nasty scars but they don't really bother me much. After a few months I go before the board of insurance examiners and let them look at me so they can determine whether or not to pay for some additional plastic surgery to reduce the scars. They poke and prod and ask me crazy questions like: Do these scars affect your self-esteem? It is several weeks before we hear that they finally agree to pay and I have another couple of quick surgeries to smooth things out and get rid of most of the scars.

This is the kind of experience mothers never want their babies to go through.

Within the year Mary finishes her classes and needs to start working full time. We don't want to put the girls into daycare so our mom moves up from Austin and takes the fourth bedroom. It's an ideal situation because mama loves taking care of her grandbabies and now we are a two-income household.

Chapter Twenty-Three

Shane's letters come almost daily and fill me with dread. He talks about when he gets out and how we'll move back to Alaska and build a log cabin. He decorates the envelopes and margins of the legal size, blue-lined pages with hearts, kisses silly words and lots and lots of exclamations points, like a twelve-year old girl with a crush. But sweet words of love and family blend right in with sentences about war and God's army and top-secret government agencies controlling his thoughts with radio waves.

Shortly after Shalyn is born I answer Shane's letters with hope and love and the possibility that maybe someday we could live that dream in Alaska. But with each passing day and week and month I know I must not do or say anything more to lead him on. I slowly change the tone of my letters as I realize we can never be a family. I try to get him to see things from my perspective and it only angers him. My new plan is to stop writing him so maybe he'll stop writing me back.

The letters interrupt my quiet life like mortar shells detonating in the kitchen. I try not to read them, but their presence begs for attention and I am always instantly sorry for giving in. His words are toxic and lethal and they usually leave me in a panic. I live in constant fear of what he can do to me even from his prison cell.

In the letters, he threatens me bodily harm, makes lewd, crude sexually explicit remarks, and rambles on for pages and pages in dull pencil that's difficult to read. Sometimes it seems he is talking to Shalyn and then sometimes to me, and then the line gets blurred and it's hard to tell who he's talking to. He usually signs them: "*Your loving husband and father*" which always leaves a bad taste in my mouth.

In an effort to move on with my life, I ignore phone calls from police agencies telling me our property that was confiscated by the DEA will be auctioned off and asking if I want to come claim any of it. I don't take the call from the officer in Anchorage who has found our Bronco at the airport with my purse inside. I instruct Daddy to tell them I'm not interested in recovering the truck or anything that might still be inside. I am so happy with my quiet little life and the welcome, normal routine we have that I don't want anything to do with anything linked to my life with Shane. I also don't want Shane to come to me looking for anything when he gets out. I don't want anything from him and I don't want him around. I just want to continue to put as much distance between us as possible.

I gave more than everything to Shane and our relationship. And now I've gotten more than everything I could have dreamed out of it with this precious child that deserves a fighting chance at a decent life. I know it's time to break the final tie; time for me to replenish my soul, rejuvenate my strength and give whatever is left inside of me to our miracle baby.

I make only one trip from Fort Worth to the Huntsville, Ellis II Unit to visit Shane the whole time he is incarcerated, and it is not the five-hour drive that keeps me from going back again. The more distance there is between me and Shane, the more clearly I see that I need to get a divorce, even though he has threatened to kill me before he will ever let that happen. But before I file the papers, I need to go look him in the eye to see if he talks in person the way he talks in his letters – to determine if he really is crazy – to make sure I'm doing the right thing.

We meet in an open courtyard picnic table area crowded with other inmates and visitors. He is very thin in his white scrub-like uniform with his last name and prison number painted over his left breast pocket, and his hair is very short. My heart is pounding so fast I can barely breathe. There are guards everywhere watching intently. He grabs me into a bear hug when he first sees me and then plants a hard, wet sloppy kiss on my surprised mouth. I am shaking all over and stunned by this sudden closeness. A guard is instantly there moving him away from me with a stern warning. Kissing is not allowed at this visit. Being in his presence brings everything rushing back and I am once again at that rest stop outside Fairbanks watching my world drive away. I am angry and hurt and spent and so over Shane. I begin to sweat and breathe heavily and I want to run. But we sit across from each other on hard metal benches; the width of the picnic table providing not nearly enough distance between us for my comfort, and I struggle to make conversation out of his choppy, erratic rambling. He grabs my hands across the table and holds them in his frantically. His fingers squeeze too tight the same way he always hugged me; not with gentle love and comfort, but like a possession to be smothered and imprisoned. My own fingers look foreign to me, enter-twined with his that I can see are yellow with nicotine stains. He never smoked cigarettes when we were together and now I am even further repulsed by him. At some point I finally manage to pull my hands free and I quickly stow them under my legs wondering how soon I'll be able to scrub them with hot, soapy water. His eyes are clear but wide and scary – they dart around constantly. He can barely sit still and doesn't make much sense. His sentences are choppy and broken just like him. I am sitting across from a wild, broken man - my husband, the father of my child. He is broken and sad and mentally ill and it is very difficult to see him this way. Gone is the strong, virile, sexy, charismatic man I fell instantly and deeply in love with so many years ago. There is nothing left of my Shane. It is an impossible hour. He wants and needs so much more from me than I can give. I cannot tell him that I love him. I cannot tell him that I miss him or that I will help him get out of prison. I cannot promise we'll be together again one day and live his dream life in Alaska, the way he begs me to over and over again. I can only share with him tiny bits and pieces about our perfect baby girl and I don't even want to give him that much. I don't want to share Shalyn with him at all. I don't want to let him into our new little world, for he will surely find a way to destroy it.

Verbatim excerpts from Shane's letters from prison:

August 1986 – May 1989.

"I want you to get your buns up here to see me or I'm going to kick your ass good for you,

Baby. Your father and I are going to go fist to fist when I get out – do you hear. I'm tired of not being able to verify the fact that my family is all right. Do you understand. I love you with all my heart. I miss you very much. Where are your letters – I'm waiting!! Write! I don't know what the problem is with your family – but you had better tell them and your attorney to go to Hell – I'm your husband and I want to see you. Get the message or I'm going to raise Hell. You would hell a lot better want me happy. I will verify where you are at all times – there is a very important reason for you to keep me informed of your safety and our daughter's safety – do you understand."

"I had to give an attitude adjustment again to a punk – got us all locked down – to hell with these bastards – your husband don't take no shit...we were watching TV but that ceased in a hurry – ha ha! I did get my point across!"

"To hell with high-tech world ways – in God's name we are going to live our lives away from all of this civilized world and get back to the basic life of love and cherish each other forever....We will have to live away from all transmission towers – away from satellite towers – frequencies are in the air everywhere they can transmit. Armageddon has begun. God bless our family! With frequencies they are putting me through hell. I need to know how you are. I am afraid of what they are programming you and little Shalyn to be or do. With these frequencies they are able to control people's minds! They can make anyone *happy or sad and do have the capabilities to program people to do things – Evil.....I want to know why you have not been to see me or written. Don't let yourself be sorry later in life. I am your husband and father of our daughter! I won't give you up or away – don't discredit yourself with me....you would be very sorry you did....Don't shame our family. WE ARE FOREVER. Don't Fuck around."*

"God's law – marriage is for eternity. I don't believe in divorce."

"I'm only trying to tell you that they (KGB) & (Secret Service of about every country on and in this planet and in space) are beating the hell out of me.....I don't know why you seem to get angry when I tell you about this damn war! You should realize your mind (brain) is being blocked! They are attacking marriages all across our country....I wish to God I'd locked you up in Alaska in the trailer or tied you to a tree at camp instead of you leading me back to Texas like a stupid dog!!!"

"Remember, the spies are watching and filming everything people do against our will and rights....Be Careful!!!"

"Baby, find out where the local nuclear fallout shelter is and if it is prepared for survival!!! All of our family needs to move into a public nuclear fallout shelter and prepare!! There will only be a

few people warned before the strike – I've been telling you that the Secret Service of the United States office of the President is transmitting to me. The space bases are at war now, the missiles are knocked out in outer space, but when the computers make a mistake the surface of the planet gets hit!!!

"Tell the church people the Federal Secret Service is transmitting to your husband by use of the Free Electron Beam Phazer-Lazer Radio – Two way radio phazer lazer."

"The Federal Government sanctions bars to promote adultery of wives and men...to destroy the family structure!! The court system denied away man's God-given law to execute wives that commit adultery."

"I'll never share you – don't cross me....I will do what I can to destroy you if I can't hold on to my family."

"There's good in you. I don't hate you. Powers were watching us before we met. A lot of things I wanted us to do together we didn't get to do because of the Powers. This place as been hard on me because of the Powers."

"I'm working in a mattress factory. I wish I could be happy. The days go by and I try to stay

out of trouble. I'm on cell restriction because of a scuffle."

"I'm no damn good – hell – I'm the man that has been a friend. Don't live that damn hating me program. I told you I owned you my woman – be with me – don't laugh at me – us – The damn world of Texas Leader Punks have damn sure made it all a damn joke."

"We are starting a Church, GOD's Church. I'm getting signatures to support our United FREE Christian's Security Force so we can help build our King, Lord Jesus Christ's Army."

"Don't leave me. You've been hateful and stupid."

"Some people I've known close haven't written. I didn't realize the <u>super natural</u> was so thick."

"I'm very sorry I was whipped so bad during this war! People have been taken hostage all over the hemisphere!"

In one surprisingly rational six-page letter that seems directed at Shalyn, he lays out his family history with dates of birth and dates of marriages and the names of his parents, all his brothers and sisters and aunts and uncles and grandparents. He says his great grandfather, at the age of 21 took a 12-year-old full-blood Indian girl off a reservation and married her. He lists "crimes" against the family that were committed by his uncle and his mother and one of his brothers. He even lists his own transgressions and crimes of adultery in our marriage.

Shane was married once before me. In this letter he tells a horrific story of what brings that marriage to an end and how he spent years running from the heartache and practically killing himself traveling all over the country, partying too much; drinking and taking too many drugs. He says that he ends up in jail in Colorado where he prayed to God for someone very special to enter into his life. Then he goes on to say that just a few days later "I met the most wonderful, special, sweetest, gorgeous, loving caring, fantastic person in the universe and fell head over hills in love with all my heart and desires, your sweet sweet mommy....and by God's blessing she honored me by becoming my wife...she made me whole and saved my soul...and for eternity I will love and cherish her."

I have never heard the details of his first marriage before. I had no idea he felt that God had brought me into his life as an answer to a prayer. Here I have been thinking all these years that he was brought into my life as my destiny and now I learn that he thinks of me as his.

I keep only a small fraction of the letters Shane writes me during this time because most of them are so vile and disgusting and they disturb me so much that I destroy them immediately so that I never have to subject myself or anyone else to the impact of his sick, twisted words again. In hindsight, I think maybe I should have kept some of the more threatening letters just so there would be proof in case anything ever happens to me or Shalyn.

On multiple occasions, he threatens to kidnap Shalyn and kill me as soon as he is released from prison. He lists ways he will torture me before I am dead. He tells me sick hideous things he wants to do with my body.

I know he is sick. I know he is not in his right mind, but I also know that he is capable of extreme violence. I have seen him beat a man to a bloody pulp with a gun. I have seen him intimidate and use people with his money and drugs. I know that he knows some bad people. I worry that he will have someone else hurt us even before he gets out of prison. All of this worry simmers on the back burner as I make my way through my days.

Meanwhile, life just keeps getting better and better in our little red house. It is such a blessing to have mama living with us and taking care of our little girls. She cooks, cleans, does the grocery shopping and keeps our little household running smoothly. Tiffany and Shalyn continue to grow and thrive. With Mary and I both working we finally have a little extra spending money for small occasional treats. We go to the movies every once in a while. We buy ice cream at the grocery store and we have everything we need.

I have even begun taking Karate lessons. The benefits more than substantiate the considerable cost as I am getting out of the house and doing something good for myself. It is great exercise and is giving me much needed self-confidence and some self-defense skills just in case Shane tries anything. At least I won't be completely helpless. I move quickly through the ranks of white, yellow, orange, green, blue and purple belts. I enjoy learning and doing the katas and even the sparring. I get pretty good and participate in tournaments, winning trophies in both categories. I am in the best physical condition of my life and am loving it. I meet new people, actually have a social life and am living more in confidence and less in fear with each passing day.

One day I am in the ring at my first tournament sporting my new brown belt and the judge has just stepped out from between my opponent and me. She is bigger than me but I am not intimidated. I am quick, skilled and confident. I jump from the starting line and throw a backhand to the right side of her face while simultaneously throwing a round kick to the left side of her head (my signature move!). I know I have just scored three points (one for the backhand and two for the kick) thus winning the round, so I drop my guard and start to turn to walk back to my line so the judges can announce the score. If I've learned anything from my sparring days, I should know better than to drop my guard. I am over confident. One judge sees the backhand but no one sees or gives me credit for the round kick so we are still sparring but I don't know this. My opponent takes advantage and throws an uppercut punch to my abdomen and knocks all the air right out of my lungs. I am down on the ground and cannot breathe. No one notices at first, but when I don't get up, someone finally comes to my aid. My coach is not here today but someone else's coach recognizes that I am in trouble and he brings me to my feet. With his hands firmly on my shoulders, he forces me to make eye contact with him and tells me to stomp my feet one at a time hard on the floor while trying to exhale at the same time. He demonstrates and does it with me while holding my shoulders and looking into my eyes. Left leg, stomp. Right leg, stomp. Left leg, stomp. Over and over until finally when I think I'm going to pass out, something lets go and I am able to suck in some air and then I am fine. I lose the match and never participate in another tournament. I rationalize this decision with the fact that I need to be more careful since I have a daughter who needs me healthy.

With all the physical conditioning bringing strength and self-confidence, I feel strong both mentally and physically. I am finally ready to file for divorce.

Chapter Twenty-Four

It is early spring 1988. Daddy is gone. He is diagnosed in the summer of 1987 with an inoperable brain tumor and dies in February 1988. His eight month illness is painful and horrific and heart wrenching to watch.

I am 27 years old. I am the single parent of a precious baby girl who will soon be two. In the past two years, I have run from the law, lost everything I owned, worked in Alaska on a cattle ranch, been in jail, given natural child birth, moved several times, started a new career, learned karate, filed for divorce from a husband that is in prison, and now my father has died.

We all later agree that daddy must have been having symptoms and dizzy spells that he kept to himself. He is home on a workday nursing a broken shoulder (after having fallen off a ladder in the garage). He is watching TV and decides he is finished. He instinctively reaches for the remote to turn off the TV but suddenly doesn't know how to work it. He is confused and knows something isn't right, so he goes to the telephone to call Donna at work but when he gets the phone in his hand, he doesn't know how to dial. When Donna comes home hours later, she finds him slumped in a corner frightened and confused.

The diagnosis is made the next day after an MRI is taken. Daddy has glioblastoma multiforme. The tumor is huge, has fingers and permeates most of his brain. They say it is inoperable, but they decide to open up his head anyway and take a look to see if there is anything they can do. After a quick look, they sew him back together and start radiation treatments to try to shrink it.

Within days Daddy can no longer communicate verbally. Most of his words come out sounding like gibberish. He hears his mangled words and sees the confusion on our faces and gives up trying. I take him to some of his radiation treatments where they zap the spot on his clean-shaven head outlined in purple marker. It is sad and surreal. In the car, I try to find interesting things to say to him that have nothing to do with his condition. I try to remain upbeat and positive, but I'm getting the feeling he doesn't want me to pretend, so mostly we ride in silence.

The drugs make him lose his hair and bloat up like a balloon and he is barely recognizable. The months pass and he continues to deteriorate. We celebrate his 51st birthday, Thanksgiving and Christmas quietly and he dies in a hospital bed in an apartment with all of us there, just a few days before my baby sister, Jeanie's wedding. Our brother-in-law, Mike, stands in and walks her down the aisle.

Shalyn will be two years old in May. I am thankful Daddy knew her, at least for a short time. Daddy was a quiet man. He never told me how to live my life....never gave me advice or asked any questions, but I know he loved me and wanted only the best for all of us. I also know he was happy that I have filed for divorce from Shane.

What should be a simple divorce is turning into a circus. After filing, my attorney receives notice from Shane's court-appointed attorney that the divorce is being contested and that there will be a trial before a judge.

It should not surprise me that Shane is fighting me on this. He has said all along that he does not believe in divorce, that marriage is eternal and that he will never let me go or share me with anyone else. I cry and fret and worry myself half to death the weeks leading up to the trial, even though my attorney assures me that the trial is just a formality...a way to give Shane an opportunity to express himself and tell his side of the story, and to go on record as not wanting the divorce. My attorney also tells me that in the state of Texas there's no way a judge is not going to grant me a divorce from a man who has been convicted of a felony. I don't understand the law. I don't trust the court system or lawyers or judges either. They have all caused me nothing but angst and misery in the past.

I find my attorney in the yellow pages. Connie goes with me for our first consultation where I tell him my story. It is the first time I tell it and it sounds fantastical even to my own ears.

I live a quiet life where only Connie and my family know what I've been through. I have this whole secret past that I'm afraid for anyone to find out about. I have a job and new friends and none of them know anything about my experiences over the past few years. I am terrified for anyone to find out for fear I will be ridiculed, fired, or who knows what else. My imagination runs wild sometimes and there is no end to the misery I can conjure in my mind. Perhaps it's all still too fresh and real to share.

But I have to tell my attorney and Connie lends much-needed moral support and helps me get through the rough parts by filling in the gaps when I become too emotional to speak. He appears un-phased by my story; he takes the case, I give him $600 (what's left of my little nest egg) and now we are going to trial.

The taxpayers are going to have to pay to have Shane driven from Huntsville to Fort Worth and back, to attend a divorce trial that is supposedly just a formality.

And then it is done.

I can't believe it! I am divorced!!! Shane's theatrics before the judge prove detrimental only to him. The judge repeatedly asks him to sit down and be quiet. He interrupts when my attorney is speaking. He jumps out of his seat (hand-cuffed and shackled) to profess his undying love for me and repeatedly states, throughout the proceeding, that he will not be divorced against his will. His attorney is clearly flustered and cannot control his client. Shane shows no respect for the court. He is agitated and unable to grasp the proper protocol for the situation. He clearly thinks that if he is loud enough and determined enough things will go his way.

The judge loses patience. She recognizes Shane is not in his right mind. It appears she is annoyed to have to deal with him at all. But she is firm, maintains control of her courtroom and cuts the proceedings very short. She does give him a chance to speak but soon realizes that he is rambling and making no sense and she just interrupts him mid-sentence, pounds her gavel and decrees the divorce granted. She leaves the courtroom, my attorney walks me back to his office and I never see Shane again.

Chapter Twenty-Five

Sometimes I still have nightmares where Shane is in control of me and my every move. His words, his smell, his heavy presence swim through my sleeping brain against my will and I wake shaken and traumatized, wondering if he will always be with me like this. Periodically, I call down to Huntsville to check the status of his sentence and to make sure he hasn't escaped or been set free to torture me. Each time I am told that because of bad behavior they have added more time to his sentence. Every couple of months I call again and it seems his sentence just keeps getting longer and longer and slowly I begin to relax so I call less and less frequently.

I work. I date. I do my karate and I continue to raise the most amazing daughter that ever lived, looking over my shoulder less and less.

One of the last letters I have from Shane is dated more than a year after the divorce. He says he has been sick the last few months and could use some help. He says that as soon as he is released he could pay me back. He says, "This is a letter letting y'all know I'm thinking of us all." And he signs it "Old Friend, Shane".

This sad letter moves me to tears and my heart aches for the man I once loved, the father of my child. Fleetingly, I am filled with the urge to jump into the car and drive to Huntsville to see him again, to let him see his baby girl and to be a family, at least for a moment. But the maturing, sober, protective mother in me knows we cannot, we must not go. It is finally time to bury that urge forever because my heart knows it is best to move on without him. My only focus now is to stay strong, do my best to raise Shalyn in a happy, healthy home, and continue to rebuild my life one step at a time.

THE END

EPILOGUE

I put more than everything I had into my relationship with Shane, and I got more than everything out of it through the birth of our miracle baby, who has taught me more about myself than I could ever have imagined. My decision to raise her as a single parent, without any contact with her father, was the right one for us. Shalyn was raised in a quiet, loving, supportive drug-free home, as a single child, but with cousins so close they were practically siblings. She has grown into a beautiful, intelligent young woman with a heart of gold and is currently pursuing a master's degree in social work. No mother could be more proud.

In 1994, after a few months of not checking with the TDC on Shane's status, I learned that he had been paroled to a halfway house in Fort Worth six months earlier (I had grown so complacent, after six years of hearing how Shane's prison behavior was only adding time to his sentence, that I began only calling once or twice a year). In one frantic phone call to his parole officer, I learned that Shane had checked in with the officer only once and had not been seen or heard from since.

I have no idea what happened to him. As far as I know, he has never tried to contact me. I often wonder if Shane made his way back to Alaska and is living the life he imagined in the last frontier.

AUTHOR'S BIO

Vanessa G. Foster married her husband, Ken, in 2000. They live in Fort Worth, Texas with their energetic half breed grand puppy, Hunter.

Made in the USA
Las Vegas, NV
26 January 2023